A PREPPER'S COOKBOOK

20 YEARS OF COOKING IN THE WOODS

DEBORAH D. MOORE

A PERMUTED PRESS BOOK

ISBN: 978-1-61868-667-1
ISBN (eBook): 978-1-61868-672-5

A PREPPER'S COOKBOOK
Twenty Years of Cooking in the Woods

Cover art by Quincy Alivio

PERMUTED PRESS

Permuted Press, LLC
275 Madison Avenue, 14th Floor
New York, NY 10016
permutedpress.com

ACKNOWLEDGEMENTS

The first thank you goes to Michael Wilson at Permuted Press for taking the chance two years ago on this unpublished author. I hope I've justified your risk.

To my sons Eric and Jason for being my recipe guinea pigs all these years. Be warned, I'm not done yet.

A special thank you goes to my friend and fellow author, David M. Salkin, author of a dozen novels, for his culinary and wine expertise in providing wine suggestions for a number of my recipes.

And last but not least, to my editor, Felicia Sullivan for fixing all the little faux pas. You are amazing.

This is for my sons, Eric and Jason, two incredible young men who inspired me and tolerated my culinary experiments. I truly could not have done this without you. You two are my finest creations and I love you deeply.

A WOMAN'S ODE TO PREPPING

I'm not into fashion
I like camouflage
I got surveillance equipment
Stashed out in my garage
I don't wear many skirts
I kinda like my jeans
And they go so much better with
My bullets and my beans.

Now don't be thinking that I'm crazy,
Not a sociopath, not even mean,
But if you come a knockin'
Keep your hands where they are seen.....

I got a Smith & Wesson,
AK and Mossberg too,
One Colt, two Beretta's,
A Kel Tech.. Hmm that one's new

I don't know when the SWHTF
But I'll let you in on a secret,
Let you in on my plan ....
I've got water, and I've got fish
I've got ammo in my pockets
And a camera in my Dish.

I got flour, sugar and my salt,
And if you don't, that's not my fault

The pantry is full of canned goods
Closets are filled up too
Everything's been inventoried
Even all my shoes.

Kerosene is for the lamp light
And matches are a must.
No one knows what I have
For there's no one that I trust.

Chickens I will raise, maybe some rabbits on my land,
And a nice big garden, to help me feed the clan
Seeds I've got, oh, ain't it nice,
I got all that *and* three kinds of rice.

I got flour, sugar and my salt,
And if you don't, that's not my fault

I don't get the hurricanes
No floods or earthquakes here,
Just lots of icy blizzard snow
And Mutant Zombie Deer.

I'm ready for a nuke blast
Solar flares or acid rain
I'm ready for the Bird Flu
When the world gets quite insane.

I've done my preps,
Checked them double twice,
Not like in Jericho
Cause folks won't be that nice.

My B.O.B. is packed
Now what did I forget?
Oh yeah, the gennie's full
And sitting on the deck.

When TEOTWAWKI is finally here,
I'll be hunkered in my retreat,
family will be near,

And I got flour, sugar and my salt,
And if you don't, that's your own damn fault.

D.D. Moore

CONTENTS

PASTAS, BREADS AND PASTRIES

VENISON, FISH AND CHICKEN

INTRODUCTION

I was a Prepper, long before the term had any meaning. As a new bride, and at the tender age of 19, I was living and working in Detroit. That winter, the area was hit with a late spring blizzard. As the child of a policeman, I was very law-abiding and fully intended to heed the warnings to stay off the streets once the snow fell so the work crews could clear the snow. To do that though, I needed more than the two cans of soup in the cupboard. I ventured to the grocery store and got caught up in the mob of shoppers who were also preparing to weather in. It took longer to check out than it did for me to shop. I vowed to never be caught that short of food ever again.

With the arrival of my first son two years later, I was suddenly responsible for this tiny person, and I took that job very seriously. I never ran out of diapers or formula, ever. I had learned my lesson. Many people have heard of a Go-Bag or a Bug Out Bag, but the very first one for me was a diaper bag. It contained not only diapers and formula but also a change of clothes, toys, blankets, snacks, water and a book for me to read. Two and a half years later, my second son was born. Concerned for our wellbeing, we moved out of Detroit to the country. I was able to have chickens and a huge garden. It was a new experience to have so much food growing fresh. I got a book on canning and taught myself the basics. The very first thing I made was jam with strawberries fresh from the garden, and as I was ladling that first scoop into a jar, it spilled over the side and burned my thumb – badly. I wrapped an ice cube around that throbbing digit and kept going. The blister was the size of my thumb nail, and it was the last time I burned myself while canning. I learn quickly. I canned, froze, and sold quite a bit of produce that year, and we never again went hungry.

The following summer my parents came to visit and my mother was appalled at my living situation. The house was an old farmhouse, but it was in good repair, freshly painted and clean, and I made sure the garden was neatly weeded. We lacked for nothing and were happy. Still, she swept her arm around my pride and joy, commenting that she had raised me so I "wouldn't have to do this." Initially I was crushed because I was doing "this" out of love for my family. Mother always had a small garden, and I had a large one. What I didn't know at the time, was that she was *forced* to tend the dozens of chickens her father raised, and she hated it. I loved it. I reveled in the knowledge that I was providing healthy food for my children with my own two hands. In the five years we lived there, my parents never came back.

Fast forward many years to a time when those young tykes were now young teens and I had divorced and remarried. We now lived in the center of the small town we had been on the outskirts of. Although I had a garden, it was not nearly as big as the one on the farm, and there were no chickens allowed, but I still provided healthy food for the four of us, and I expanded my knowledge of canning. My preparedness never faltered; I never had less than two months of food available for us.

I neglected most of my own personal needs and desires in favor of raising my sons well, and being a good wife. After the boys left home to be on their own, as all children are meant to do, I once again took up writing as a way to fulfill some of my emptiness, and only partially succeeded. I grew restless. New horizons and a new life called to me.

I moved to the woods of the Upper Peninsula of Michigan to start over with a new mate, Pete, who shared my desire for a simpler life. A new, efficient house set in the center of one hundred and sixty acres of land, powered only by four large solar panels, a wood burning furnace in the walkout basement, a new wood burning cookstove in the kitchen and a *real* icebox: totally off-grid. I had found home.

All that land gave me the room to do anything. My garden grew to 100′ x 150′, protected only by a solar charged electric fence. I had a few mishaps, though it produced enough to keep us fed. After the first very harsh winter that I was mentally unprepared for, I realized that chickens would not fare well in my new setting. They would have to wait.

That first summer we worked long hours to finish the house that had only been closed in the previous fall. A bare stud interior delighted the cats, though that didn't last long. We wired, did plumbing, and hung drywall. He taped and mudded the drywall seams and I sanded. Then I painted, did the trim work and laid the tile carpeting. By November we had moved in all of the furniture we had in storage. We took days off from working on the house to cut firewood. Lots and lots of firewood. I still have no idea how I knew to do some of the things I did, but by the end of October, I had stored enough kindling to supply both the wood stove and the wood furnace. Winter was coming.

The first winter was a true learning experience. Although we had shelves in the basement for food storage, and a month or so of food, I had not considered that I wouldn't be able to resupply easily. When the snow hit, we parked one vehicle out at the main road. At over a mile into the woods it would be impossible to plow that distance. We had one old snowmobile that I didn't know how to drive, so I would snow shoe out to the car, pulling a sled. I learned that a full sled on the return trip was very heavy to pull over a mile. From that time on, my pantry was full by November, with enough to last us eight months, while I could still drive the supplies in. Grocery shopping after that was simple fresh vegetables or meat, or just a reason to get out of the woods.

Cooking on the wood stove came easily to me, as I love to cook. I had to adjust my timing a great deal and nothing was instant. I will go into detail later, but suffice to say I reveled in the new method. One of the activities I clung to during the winter was writing magazine articles on off grid living, cooking, and storage. It quickly became a satisfying refuge for me. Not only writing though, I also made my own clothes on my treadle sewing machine, did embroidery, along with basic knitting and crocheting, hand painted our Christmas cards and... I cooked. I set up menus for weeks in advance, trying new recipes cut from culinary periodicals. I would try something new, change it, adjust it to our taste until it became my own. I experimented with baking, creating new and unusual breads. I kept a notebook on everything I tried and rated it. Some things became favorites, others were never made again.

The second summer I took a weekend class on mushroom foraging, which I still do whenever the season is right. I bought books on wild edibles, and to this day, supplement my food with wild cattail flowers, ramps, fiddleheads and of course, a variety of mushrooms. I even dabbled in growing mushrooms on logs; what fun *that* was.

Having paid cash for everything, the land, the house and everything it took to finish it so we could remain debt-free, the money ran out a year later and I went back to work. The work was summer seasonal and trying to keep up with work, the garden, and the canning exhausted me. I would physically and mentally recover over the winter, but after several years it became increasingly difficult. It's impossible to have a goal that takes two when only one is committed to it.

When Y2K happened, I doubled the stock in the pantry. He was furious that I would even consider something would happen and I was just as angry that he didn't.

We lasted seven years. After selling the house in the woods, I reinvested my share in a smaller house, on ten wooded acres, outside of the same small town and still in the woods.

I lived the life. I still do.

I kept my wood cookstove and it still heats my house all winter, providing me with a ready cooking surface and a hot oven to bake. I still have to store just as much wood, about fourteen face cord, and I do it by myself in the spring so it can cure and dry all summer. I also do it early because I don't want to worry about my winter wood supply while I'm busy working, gardening, and canning. Priorities have to be set and abided by. If you fail to plan, you plan to fail. Having a plan without a goal is senseless; having a goal without a plan is worthless.

My garden is now 25′ × 85′ and is protected with a high fence topped with a grid electric charger. It's easy to maintain, even with my busy summer work schedule, and provides me with enough food to eat fresh, can for storage, and to share with my family. My pantry is still filled by November first and has increased over the years. A good Prepper never admits to how much they have stored, but I could last a very long time without shopping. It's actually a relief to be able to stock up on what I know is necessary without someone questioning or criticizing my every move.

Attached to the big barn I had built is the chicken coop, with a dozen well fed and happy chickens. Finally. They provide eggs daily and meat occasionally. The rooster ensures I have fertile eggs to incubate to perpetuate the flock.

I have reconnected with my artistic side and do watercolor painting now, and with five new published novels, my writing dream has come true.

And I cook.

I cook from my pantry. Every recipe in this book I can make at any given time. A well-stocked, well planned pantry provides that for me. Do I have cans of crab meat for the stuffed ziti? Absolutely. Do I have anchovy paste for the Caesar salad? I wouldn't be without it. As you browse through these recipes, remember, yes, I really do have everything on hand to make every dish.

THE WORKING PANTRY
VS.
THE RETREAT PANTRY

Whereas a *retreat* pantry is for long term, the *working* pantry is for right now, tomorrow, next week, and next month. What to have in the working pantry is a very personal thing, it will always depend on what you and your family like, can, will and do eat. Does your family love peanut butter? Then stock up on the big jars and rotate. Do they like it just sometimes? Then go for the smaller jars and rotate. Anyone allergic? Don't even keep it in the house, no matter what anyone says about how good the protein is.

Dried herbs fit the working pantry. The retreat pantry has the herbs growing in the garden, the working pantry has them dried on the shelf, ready to use in the middle of winter. Because I live at my retreat, I have both types of pantries.

How does one know what to stock and how much is the topic for many discussions. A retreat pantry is for the next six years, a working pantry is for the next six months. The working pantry can have more short term foods, items that have an expiration of less than two years, plus dried foods, convenience foods and experimental items. Experimental items are those your family or you haven't tried yet, or haven't had much of. Items that you may decide you really don't like are not items you want to have a case of. That would be a waste of money, space, and effort.

One of the most effective ways to stock a working pantry is to save receipts from shopping. Save them all for a month, check what you tend to buy. Make a list of favorite foods and watch for sales. Once you have a list of what you use, like, and buy for a month, extrapolate for the next six months, stock, then rotate. Don't forget to add the occasional items, like spices or exotic foods. Use one tube of anchovy paste every two or three months? Always have two or three on hand. Never use it? Keep one, as you never know when a recipe may call for it, but only after you've stocked everything normally used by your family.

There will be items that can't be pre-stocked for six months, like potato chips, but you can stock up for a week or two, or stock up on popcorn instead! Expand your thinking and always take advantage of sales.

Pantries will often include non-food items, so don't forget those: aluminum foil, parchment, plastic baggies, wax paper, disposable foil pans, and paper plates. These are kitchen/cooking oriented items, not to be confused or included with other paper products.

Suggestions for items you might not always stock, but will be needed during an 'event': flour, sugar, salt, seasonings, oil, biscuit mix (for quick biscuits and pancakes), mac & cheese, ramen-style noodles, evaporated milk, bullion, pasta, rice, meat (tuna, corned beef, chicken, spam), drink flavoring (Tang, Kool-Aid), water.

Once you get your pantry stocked with what you and your family use, it's easier to maintain. Remember - rotate, rotate, rotate! And whatever you do, don't forget the family pet!

THE RETREAT FOOD STORAGE

There are many, many articles on food storage to be found on the net, mine included. Back in 1998, *Country Side Magazine* published my lengthy article on how I did my pantry inventory. The article is still on their website for viewing. Keeping in mind this was pre-Y2K and pre-internet for me, and I did everything manually. It was simple and it worked and it's been copied many times. Flattering!

That was my home pantry, my every day usage food stock, so now I'd like to take it a step further, and discuss how to stock your retreat pantry. For most, their retreat is NOT where they live. It was for me then, it is for

me now, but since I have a different view of life these days, I think of here as my retreat first, home second.

If your retreat is 'someplace else', your food storage *must* be different. This food is not in constant rotation as your home pantry is, so it must be viewed for longer term. Keep in mind the well-used saying: Store what you eat, eat what you store. There is little reason to stock a ton of rice if you don't like it, or if you're allergic to it, even though rice is one of the best things to store long term. Select what you *like*. Want flour for making bread? Don't store flour, store wheat. Go back to the origin. The exception to the rule of storing only what you eat, would be for others in your collective, or for bartering.

My suggestions for long term retreat storage includes: rice, wheat, sugar, dried beans, salt, bouillon, a variety of grains (barley, millet, oats), pasta, freeze dried yeast, cooking oil, vinegar, coffee, powdered milk, instant/dried potatoes, anything dried, especially vegetables. All of these should be packed in plastic buckets, sealed with 02 absorbers. Might not stop all mice, but it sure will slow them down.

Some would suggest herbs and spices. Spices yes, herbs no. Herbs degrade quickly, so plant them around the retreat instead, and dry them when they're harvested. Store spices in glass jars, including peppercorns, cinnamon, allspice, nutmeg, cloves, and mustard seed. Spices should be purchased whole, not in powdered form, and ground as needed. Done that way, they will last indefinitely. I always keep bottles of lime juice and lemon juice on hand just in case I can't get fresh ones. Don't forget flavor extracts such as vanilla, lemon, orange, and almond. Choose any flavors that your family likes. They can go a long way to making a dish more normal during a not so normal time.

The next thing I would add would be canned meats. Though they will not last as long as dried foods, they can have long shelf lives, so check the dates carefully. Again, stock variety: tuna, salmon, mackerel, corned beef, chicken, beef, pork, bacon.

Chicken, beef, pork, and bacon can be home canned and the shelf life extended.

Next in line would be canned vegetables, fruits, condiments. For long term, these are the least desirable and the most vulnerable to spoilage, so don't depend on them.

A vital key to base storage foods is knowing what to do with them, so don't forget to learn how to make bread, bagels, cornbread, along with ketchup, mustard, and jams.

One more thought about disaster storage. I rely very little on a freezer, because if the power grid goes down, losing all that food can be a disaster in itself. In the freezer I store only meats that can be canned and butter, lots of butter. I keep twelve pounds on hand all the time, and if kept cool it will last a very long time. Mostly I can my produce in jars. I highly recommend taking a class through your extension service and getting a good guide book, such as a Ball or Kerr book on canning. Home canned produce lasts a very long time, but don't forget to rotate it. Home canned is stored in the house so won't be subjected to weather and temperature fluctuations, and requires nothing more than opening: no thawing, no rehydrating. Dehydrating foods is another means of preserving that can be safely subjected to temperature changes, however, it requires water to make it edible, which may be in short supply. Personally, I dry very few foods. My favorite though, is corn. Adding a handful to a pot of soup adds extra flavor and nutrients, and is a simple way to rehydrate it.

My friend David M. Salkin is a wine aficionado, and has agreed to add a wine suggestion to some of the more gourmet dishes. Most wines store very well.

Mixed in with the recipes, I've included stories from my life deep in the woods. I hope you find them interesting.

One final comment about the recipes. Some of them I have had for so long, I don't know the original source.

Let's get cooking!

SOUPS, SNACKS AND SALADS

SOUPS

Scraps of Useable Parts

FRENCH ONION

This sounds exotic and complicated, but it isn't. I managed to coerce a secret from a chef about how he made this fabulous soup. What was his secret? The stock. It was started in the morning and *everything* went into it. The celery tops, onion peels, carrot ends and peelings, potato peels, lots of beef and chicken trimmings, green pepper and tomato cores— whatever he was doing that day went in, and was cooked and then strained out the next day. So of course it's really hard to duplicate, even for him. Try it someday, it's worth the extra time. If I know it's going to be a busy day in the kitchen, I'll put a pot of water on the back of the stove and keep adding to it. The next day I have some awesome stock. Oh, and slow cooking the onions is really important here.

- 4 T. butter
- 4 T. olive oil
- 8 cups onion* thinly sliced
- 8 cups of beef broth
- ½ cup white wine
- 1 tsp. fresh black pepper
- 1 tsp. salt
- Shredded Swiss cheese and croutons

* For an interesting taste use a combination of red, white and yellow, and wild ramps

Melt the butter and oil in a deep soup pot. Add onions and stir to coat well. Cover and simmer on low for 20 minutes. Remove cover and cook at medium for another 45 minutes, stirring frequently. The onions will turn transparent. Be careful not to burn them. Add beef stock and wine and cook another 45 minutes. Add salt and pepper, adjusting to taste.

Ladle soup into individual bowls, add a few croutons, cover with Swiss cheese, and place under broiler for a few minutes to melt and brown. Serve immediately. Not having a broiler, I put the bowls in the wood stove oven until the cheese melts. French bread is a must for this soup.

Scraps **O**f **U**seable **P**arts = **SOUP**!

PASTA E FAGIOLI

My mother loved an Italian restaurant near where she lived, and I would always take her there for lunch when I would come to town for a visit. Pronounced *pasta fa-zool*, this was her favorite soup. My sister Pam and I continued this tradition when I would visit after mom passed. During one visit, Pam and I ate our soup very slowly, trying to pick out the ingredients, and this is what we came up with.

- 1 can northern beans
- 1 can kidney beans
- 1 cup celery, diced
- 1 large onion, diced
- 1 cup carrots, diced
- 1 pound ground beef
- 2 quarts home canned tomatoes, crushed
- 1 T. chili powder, or to taste
- 3 T. brown sugar, or to taste
- 1 tsp. crushed red pepper flakes, or to taste
- Pasta: small shells, bow ties, or any small pasta, cooked firm
- Beef broth*

Brown the ground meat in a medium size pot. Drain any fat. Add in the beans (do not drain), celery, onion, carrots, and tomatoes. Stir and bring to a boil, then reduce to a simmer. Add the chili powder and red pepper flakes and simmer for 1 hour. Taste; if the soup has too much of a tomato taste, add the brown sugar, one tablespoon at a time. Simmer another 1 hour.

Serve over the pasta. I prefer to put some pasta in a soup bowl and ladle in the soup, that way the pasta doesn't get over cooked.

* To stretch the soup further, add 1 cup to 1 quart of beef broth, as desired.

MOM'S TALARINI

While not really a soup, this is soupy and needs to be served in a bowl. It also goes by different names. The most common is Italian Delight, but I know it best by what my mother called it: Talarini (*Tal-a-ree-knee*). The different ingredients have a wonderful way of complementing each other while staying separate to the taste.

- 1 pound ground meat
- 1 medium onion, chopped
- 1 can whole corn, with the juice
- 1 can sliced black olives, with the juice
- 1 quart tomatoes, with juice
- 1 package dry noodles
- 1 pound Longhorn/Colby cheese, chunked

Brown the burger with the onion and drain off the fat. Add corn, olives, and tomatoes. Bring to a boil. Add the noodles. Reduce heat and simmer until the juice is absorbed by the dry noodles. Add the cheese and heat just until cheese melts. It's that simple.

Serve hot in soup bowls.

SPECIAL MOMENTS...

BUTTERFLIES

One spring, I had noticed an abundance of butterflies congregating at my bridge. Fluted Swallowtails, the yellow and black butterflies, gentle, pretty, and prolific. It seemed that there was a depression in the road where it was damp, and was prime for something they enjoyed. Never did figure out what it was. The butterflies were everywhere! They were also in the middle of the road.

I really hated driving over them, I couldn't help but kill a few, and I felt bad doing that. That one day, as I approached the bridge, there were literally hundreds of the black and yellow wings, pulsating. I slowed, wondering what to do, then had an idea. I slowly rolled over the area and stopped. Startled, the butterflies took off. Suddenly I was encompassed in black and yellow wings!! Hundreds enveloped the car, I was surrounded by their beauty. I was giddy with awareness of being the center of their activity.

I sat there for a few minutes, awestruck by what had just happened. I was hoping they would leave unharmed, but they gave me an incredible gift, a moment in nature. Butterflies are symbolic of transformation, and although I did not understand it at that time, I now see how much I treasure that memory, and how it has transformed my perception of beauty in even the smallest creature.

* * *

HARVEST CHOWDER

Soups and chowders are very similar. The difference, to me, is that chowder usually has a creamy base to it. Soups and chowders that come from the garden can contain almost anything, so there are endless variations.

- 6 pieces bacon, chopped
- 1 green pepper, chopped
- 1 large onion, chopped
- 3 carrots, diced
- 4 large potatoes, scrubbed and diced
- ½ tsp. fresh thyme
- 1 T. fresh basil
- 1 tsp. salt Fresh ground pepper to taste
- 1 quart chicken broth
- 1 can evaporated milk or 1 pint whole milk

Brown the bacon until crispy. Add green pepper and onion, cooking until tender. Add chicken broth and bring to a boil. Add potatoes, carrots, and any other vegetables you've selected, plus the herbs, salt and pepper. Cook until vegetables are tender. Stir in milk and heat. Serve in warmed bowls with hot biscuits.

OPTIONS: *Jerusalem artichokes (scrubbed and diced), corn off the cob, summer squash, green beans, peas, basically anything fresh from the garden, cut into bite sized pieces.*

NOTES: *for clam chowder, add a can of clams before the milk.*

FISH CHOWDER

My father said I could bait a hook before I could tie my shoes. Consequently, I love to go fishing. Fishing is not necessarily catching these days, but it's more fun if I can bring home enough fish for a meal and even better if there is enough to can too. Canning fish, whether caught or purchased when the price is low, is also a wise moneysaving venture. Of course, I can't fry canned fish, but this chowder is a stunning use of what you might have in storage and is different enough from the Harvest Chowder to warrant its own recipe.

- 6 slices bacon, chopped
- 1 large onion, finely diced
- 1 clove garlic, minced or crushed
- 1 quart tomatoes
- 4 large potatoes, peeled and cubed
- 1 pint jar whole corn (or one can)
- 1 bay leaf
- 1 tsp. basil
- 1 pint jar fish (or one pound fresh fillets)
- 1 can evaporated milk (or one pint whole milk)
- Salt and pepper to taste

In a large pot or Dutch oven, cook the bacon until crisp, then add onions and garlic and sauté until soft. Add the tomatoes and bring to a boil. Add the potatoes, corn and herbs. Cook until potatoes are tender. Add fish and cook additional 10 minutes. Stir in milk and heat. Remove the bay leaf. Serve with a crusty bread.

GUMBO

Gumbo is one of those thick soups, almost a stew— a *stewp* — and it's always better after it has simmered all day. If I know I have someone coming over after noon but am not sure when, this is the perfect meal to have available staying warm on the back of the stove. The rice can be fixed last minute since it usually takes a half hour or so to say hi.

- 1 pound bulk spicy sausage (I often use venison sausage and add some canned bacon)
- 1 large onion, chopped
- 1 green pepper, chopped
- 2 cans okra
- 1 quart jar tomatoes
- 2 cloves garlic, minced
- 1 tsp. fresh ground pepper
- 1 tsp. Worcestershire sauce
- Dash of tabasco
- 1 T. balsamic vinegar
- White rice, cooked
- Seafood optional (shrimp, crawdads, or chunks of fish)

Brown the sausage (and bacon if using) until cooked, breaking into small pieces, add the onion, green pepper, and garlic, sauté until limp. Add the rest of the ingredients except for the rice and optional seafood. Add the seafood at the end, (while cooking the rice) and heat thoroughly.

To serve, place a scoop of rice in a bowl and ladle gumbo on top. Add some sourdough bread and you've got an unforgettable meal.

SPECIAL MOMENTS...

HAWK

Early one misty Fall morning, I was driving out our road, heading for the main route that would take me to town, totally preoccupied with events in my life. Suddenly, a large bird swooped low in front of me. As I hit the brakes, it rose again, but dropped something. I thought perhaps it had been carrying something in its talons and I was curious. But it wasn't something that had been carried, it was a large feather, perhaps from the tail or wing. Overall, the feather measured 9" long - from a red-shouldered hawk! A gift, left right in my path. Of course I kept it. I felt the hawk meant that feather for me, and was trying to tell me something. I had been studying the symbolism of animals in Native American culture. The area I live in is strongly influenced by the Ojibwa culture, and I do believe I could feel ancient spirits still clinging to my woods. The hawk is a Watcher, and was telling me to be aware of my surroundings.

* * *

CHICKEN NOODLE

Here in the woods, I like to use the freshest ingredients possible for whatever it is I'm cooking. My first choice for this recipe would be to go out to the barn and kill a chicken, though I realize that's not an option for most people.

- 1 whole chicken, cut up
- 2-3 quarts boiling water
- 2 celery stalks, coarsely chopped
- 2 onions, coarsely chopped
- 1 tsp. whole peppercorns
- 1 sprig each parsley, basil, thyme
- 6 leaves of sage
- 1 bay leaf

After straining the broth add:

- 1 carrot, finely diced
- 1 medium onion, finely diced

Homemade pasta, wide cut (if you are using prepared/dried pasta from your food storage, use wide cut egg noodles)

Wash chicken, cut up, and place in a large pot with boiling water. Bring back to a boil and add remaining ingredients except for the carrot, onion, and pasta. Cook for 2 hours, until chicken is well done. Place a large colander over another pot and strain. Set chicken to cool. Defat broth and return to pot, and continue cooking down.

When the chicken has cooled enough to handle, remove meat from the bones. (Bones, skin, and vegetables can be pressure cooked later for the dog.) Return meat to the broth, add the carrot and onion; cook until tender. Add cooked homemade pasta noodles (or dried/prepared pasta – cooked). Adjust to taste with salt and pepper.

NOTE: *If you don't have one of those handy measuring cups with the spout at the bottom that lets you separate fat, set the pot in the refrigerator or outside to cool and the fat will harden, making it easy to lift off.*

EGG DROP SOUP

I was amazed once I how easy this soup is to make at home. All you need to know is how. With the abundance of fresh eggs, I have this often.

- 1 quart chicken broth
- 1 T. soy sauce
- 2 T. cornstarch
- ¼ cup water
- 2 eggs, beaten
- 1 green onion finely chopped, greens included (or use chives)

Bring the chicken broth and soy sauce to a simmer over medium heat. Mix the cornstarch and water together and add to broth, stirring constantly until slightly thickened. Raise the heat and slowly add the eggs, continuing to stir, but slowly. Top with green onions. Serve.

Would you ever have guessed it was that easy?

ERIC'S TURTLE SOUP

When the boys were young, we lived on the mill pond of a small town. My oldest, in his teens, was always looking for something to earn extra money, and started trapping and selling the snapping turtles that were plentiful. One buyer shared this recipe for soup with him.

- 1 pound turtle meat, cut into small pieces
- 2 quarts beef or chicken stock
- 1 tsp. salt
- 2 T. butter
- 1 large onion, chopped
- 2 T. flour
- 1 quart tomatoes
- 1 clove garlic, chopped
- 1 tsp. fresh ground pepper
- 1 tsp. Worcestershire sauce

Bring turtle meat, stock, and salt to a boil, then simmer for 2-3 hours, until the meat is tender. Brown the onions in butter, then blend in flour. Add some juice from the tomatoes to the flour mixture, and then add to the soup, blending well. Add the tomatoes, garlic, pepper, and Worcestershire sauce. Simmer another 30 minutes.

One summer, my son caught a rather large snapper that swallowed the hook. In trying to get it into the cage, he needed my help. I held the cable fish line, and it took everything I had to keep it from biting him! I was shocked by the strength of that turtle!

LEARNING TO COOK ON A WOODSTOVE

When I began my transition period of moving to and living in the woods, I also began a period of education. I bought books and magazines and took classes on everything from solar collecting to gardening.

One subject evaded me: cooking on a wood-burning stove. Every time I saw a magazine that flashed headlines on wood stoves, my hands would tremble in anticipation as I reached for it. However, the wood stoves in question were for heating, not for cooking.

Since I was looking at a self-sufficient lifestyle and wood on my 160 acres was virtually free, there wasn't even a consideration to use anything but wood for heating and cooking. My land was approximately ninety-five percent maple, a steady source of excellent quality hardwood.

Initially, I tried to find a real antique stove for my kitchen. Since the 20′ × 24′ kitchen/dining/living room was to be the main focus of our new house, I wanted the stove not only to be functional, but attractive as well. The antique stoves I found were either attractive and of questionable functionality, or functional and downright ugly.

I bit the bullet and bought a brand-new, old-fashioned looking stove from an Amish store in Ohio. To this day, I'm glad I spent the extra money. Not that there aren't good old stoves out there, but I never found one.

My stove has a warming oven overhead, a tip-down butter warmer, a washable porcelain clad oven with thermostat, and an optional water jacket. The firebox has a side lifter lid and easily takes a 20-inch log. *And* it looks good.

But I still didn't know how to cook on it.

Being an experienced cook, I figured I was tough. I was smart! I was inventive! I could do this!

I was totally lost. I learned the hard way, by trial and error, lots of practice, and even more patience. I've burned a few things, but only because I wasn't paying attention.

The functioning of the stove is really quite simple. They will last for generations with proper care, since there is so little that can go wrong with them.

One end has a firebox, and outside the firebox are vents. Mine has four "dials" which regulate how much air is fed to the fire. The more you open the vents, the hotter the fire. The ash door can also be opened for a surge of air, but this needs to be watched very carefully.

There is a sliding mechanism towards the back of the firebox, which diverts the smoke coming from the fire to go around the oven box before it escapes up the chimney. This heats the oven more consistently. The position of the slide unit is most important before lighting the stove.

Because a draft needs to be created when first firing up, the slide needs to be directed to the chimney. The positioning for my stove is to the right to light, to the left to bake. If you forget to reposition the slide, the result will be a roomful of smoke.

The most important thing to remember is this: *You can't set it at 350° and walk away!* The biggest challenge is keeping the oven heat even. Unlike a gas or electric stove, when you put something in the oven to cook and the temperature drops as the food absorbs the heat, nothing kicks in to compensate. You then have to feed the firewood that will burn quickly and offer more heat.

As the food begins to cook and its internal temperature rises, a longer, slower-burning piece of wood will maintain the heat. Open the oven door if it gets too hot - but not for long. Your oven may even have "hot spots" like mine. During baking, I turn bread or cookies 180 degrees halfway through the baking time. Stay in the kitchen when there is cooking to be done. In winter, it's the best place to be.

Range top cooking is similar to a gas or electric stove, but you have more room available. The entire surface is hot, not just four little burners. Those circles are not burners, as I once thought. They are for checking on the fire.

The surface area can be divided into three major temperature zones. The hottest is right over the firebox, whether it is on the right or left. The next warmest would be in the center, and the coolest is the front of the side opposite the firebox. After the coffee perks over the firebox, it stays warm sitting on the far right corner.

Everything needs to be watched carefully, as the heat can drop or flare in a very short time. Don't be discouraged. Once you get used to the heat always being there (it doesn't shut off with the twist of a knob), cooking on a wood stove is easy.

Though it takes some patience, grilling can be done. You can get pretty good results by removing one of those little circles over the firebox and placing a heat-resistant grate over the flame. I use half of a hamburger basket meant for grilling. I also lay aluminum foil around the opening to keep splatters to a minimum. Most barbecuing is done inches above hot coals, so some adjustment is necessary. I let flames do the grilling rather than coals. Since the grate is so much further from the heat, I use a hotter fire. Although using an outdoor grill is much nicer, it's difficult when the wind is blowing snow.

The cleaning and care you give your woodstove is important. Most cook stoves have three types of surfaces. There is cast iron, porcelain, or enamel-finished sheet metal, and decorative trim. A wet rag or sponge wiped daily on the decorative trim should suffice. For baked-on spots, a bit of non-abrasive cleanser (baking soda, which should be in your preps!) works very well. Prevention is the best approach to cleaning. Avoid spilling or splashing, since you can't wipe it up right away.

Don't ever put a wet pot on the stove. Remember, the surface is cast iron and will rust, even when hot. The least of your cleaning worries will be the rust ring, but the worst will be the ring underneath the rust that is there forever. Spots that are left on too long will pit the cast iron. By first taking a razor blade to spills, you can scrape up lots of gunk and save your buffing pad and shoulder.

Scotch Brite Very Fine© is a metal sanding pad that is unsurpassed for cleaning even the toughest spots on cast iron surfaces. Always buff back and forth in one direction, from front to back, or you will get a scratched look. Always let the surface cool before buffing, or you will melt the cleaning pad.

Once the entire surface has been buffed, use a soft flannel cloth and wipe a thin layer of cooking oil over the whole surface. This seasons the top and makes it easier to clean the next day.

A word of caution: The oil has to be spread thinly. I've used too much, and when I lit the stove the next morning, the kitchen smelled like cooking popcorn.

When necessary, you will need to wipe down the metal backsplash and warming oven. Warm, soapy water or a non-abrasive cleanser will do the trick. Clean the soot from under the oven monthly in the summer and weekly in the winter when the stove is constantly running. There is a small opening concealed by a decorative nameplate directly under the oven. Use a long-handled scraper to remove the blackish soot and hardened chunks. It's best to do this when the stove is cool, or the draft will keep pulling the soot back in. Don't forget the sides of the ash compartment. Cinders don't always fall into the ash pan.

One of the most overlooked areas for cleaning is the top of the oven box. Remember, you keep diverting smoke around the oven. If enough ash collects there, it will have an insulating effect, and the oven won't heat properly. A friend and neighbor (around here, a neighbor is anyone who lives less than 10 miles away) complained that her recently purchased antique stove was giving her fits when she tried to maintain a steady temperature. I didn't hear another complaint after making this suggestion.

The cooking surface is made up of two to four panels of cast iron. Remove these panels when the stove is cold and set them on newspapers, as they are sooty. This exposes the top of the oven box. The first time I did this was after a year of cooking, and I had over two inches of ash. Carefully brush this ash into the firebox, where it can fall into the ash pan. Do this too quickly and you'll raise an ash cloud.

Then take your long-handled scraper and scrape the sides of the oven box. Soot will fall to the bottom, where it can be removed through that little hidden door. The whole process should take about 15 minutes, and it will make a world of difference in your oven temperature. This cleaning should be done bimonthly in the summer and weekly in the winter.

The gasket around the top of the stove should be carefully inspected every year and replaced if it is too worn. I never concerned myself with the gasket. Two and a half years later, there was no gasket left! My stove had lost its air tightness, and I didn't know why.

Most gasket packages I've seen include 84 inches of material, but my stove requires 100 inches. There is no loss of efficiency when material is pieced together. Just scrape the old stuff off, lightly sand, wipe off, glue and install the new gasket. This takes only 15 minutes and a few dollars, but what a difference it makes. It's always wise to keep a few gaskets in storage. You never know if they'll be available in a few years.

Cast iron pots and pans are nice, but certainly not necessary for wood stove cooking. Ceramic casserole dishes are great. Use common sense with pots that have plastic or wooden handles. Don't put anything into the oven that wouldn't go into a conventional oven, and don't position handles over the cooking area that you couldn't expose to a gas burner. Never put a plastic bowl on the stove, even if you think it's cold.

I purchased two pieces of cast iron cookware for $5 at an estate sale one summer. They were valued at over $80 new in a catalog. The old pieces cleaned up quickly and are among my favorites. One major advantage of cast iron is that it stays hot. That might not seem like a big deal until you serve a pot of stew or spaghetti on a cool evening.

Use the warming oven to your advantage. I keep two plates and two soup bowls in my warmer. Having a pre-warmed plate at mealtime can make a big difference. I also have a biscuit stone—a terra cotta disk that is heated and put in the bottom of a basket of biscuits or rolls—that I rarely remember to heat up on time, so I just leave it in the bottom of the oven.

What I cook since I first moved to the woods has changed, but that's because I've changed the way I eat. I eat less meat and more home-grown vegetables, more soups and bread. I now have the time to bake, and homemade, fresh-baked bread tastes like heaven. Soup is easy to simmer on the cookstove.

I have very little waste, because everything goes into a soup jar. This is something every cook can do. If you open a can of mushrooms, pour the juice into a jar and freeze it. After you cook vegetables, pour that liquid into the jar. I even save the liquid from soaking the roasting pan. To prevent overeating, put the last few mouthfuls of veggies, rice, or potatoes in the soup jar. It makes for some very interesting, economical, healthy and work-free soup. For me, it's a conscientious thing to do, as I care about not wasting things. In difficult times, food may become scarce.

Here in the Upper Peninsula, the weather is fairly cool or downright cold most of the time, so the stove is always running except in mid-summer, from June through September. The first thing I do in the morning is light the stove. While the kindling is catching, I feed the cat. Then I add three or four pieces of wood, light the kerosene lamp, check the temperature outside, and add larger logs to the fire. Now it's time to put the coffeepot over the firebox. Then it's back to the warmth of the bed. It takes about twenty minutes for the water to boil and another twenty to perk. By the time the coffee is ready, the room is also warm.

I bake something almost every day in the winter. Since my refrigeration (an antique ice box) is limited, I bake only one loaf of bread at a time. Cookies and biscotti are favorites around here. Dinner is usually started around 4 P.M., and after that I let the fire go out. The coals are ready to be knocked down into the ash pan by 9:00. Since I don't want to mess with all the details when it's cold in the morning, I lay a new fire, clean the stovetop and fill the coffee pot at night. I'm ready for a new day.

SNACKS

SALSA

The first time I had real salsa was in Mexico at a little open café on the side of a mountain overlooking the Pacific. The salsa was 50/50 onions and chopped tomatoes and heavy on the cilantro. It was awesome.

My favorite way to have salsa is with corn chips. This is also a prime addition when I make tortillas, page 47. In fact, there is nothing that beats still warm tortillas rolled up with some salsa inside, secure with toothpicks and sliced.

- 1 quart jar tomatoes drained well (don't forget to reserve the juice for soup!) OR one pound fresh tomatoes, cored, chopped and drained
- 1 onion finely diced
- 1 green pepper finely diced
- 1-2 jalapeño peppers, seeded and finely diced (how many will depend on how much heat you like, and the size. You can always add more.)
- 1 clove crushed garlic
- 1 T. lime juice (preferably fresh squeezed)
- 1 T. olive oil
- 1-4 T. cilantro, chopped

Mix the garlic and lime juice in a medium bowl. Add the onion, green pepper, jalapeño peppers, and oil. Stir. Add the tomatoes and toss. The amount of cilantro is to personal taste. Start out slow. Blend well and chill. This is best if allowed to mellow a few hours before serving, but still good if served immediately.

CORN CHIPS

These are actually corn tortillas cut into the wedges we are more familiar with and salted. After frying, they can also be folded in half to become the kind of taco we think of.

- 2 eggs
- ½ tsp. salt
- 5 ½ T. corn meal
- ¾ cup cornstarch
- 1 cup milk, room temperature
- 2 T. melted butter

Beat the eggs and salt together. Add the corn meal and mix well. In a medium bowl, combine the cornstarch and milk and beat to form a smooth batter. Add the egg mixture and mix until smooth. Add the melted butter and stir constantly. Grease a griddle or fry pan and pour a small amount of the batter in the center, making a thin circle. How much batter will depend on what you plan on making with them. When the tortilla is brown on one side, turn it over and brown on the other side. These should be very thin, like a crepe.

While they are warm, either cut into wedges and salt for chips, or gently fold in half for tacos.

SPECIAL MOMENTS...

OWLS

There is nothing more delightful than to hear owls calling to each other in the dark of the night. The *who-who, who whoooo* in the distance, answered by the same but closer call, has always brought a smile to me. It is a reassurance that all is well. The owls are watching over the night.

One very cold, snowy afternoon, right at dusk, there was movement that caught my attention. I had to look very closely, but I could see the Snowy Owl that had just perched in a tree overlooking the clearing next to the house. It was magnificent! Sitting perfectly still, it was at least two feet tall, and blended in with the snow covered branches. As night fell, it got more and more difficult to see this incredible bird, but it was still there, still sitting patiently. The clearing was also where the bird feeder was, and although the birds weren't out at night, the rodents were. The mice crept up through their tunnels at night to scrounge all the seeds the birds had dropped during the day, and the owl knew this. Just as it was almost too dark to see, the Snowy Owl left its perch, diving for the ground and then back up. It took my breath away. The wing span was at least four feet across, perhaps more, and completely silent. The sight was another gift from nature.

* * *

CHEESY CRACKERS

These are also called Penny Snacks, probably because they resemble a penny that has been flattened on railroad tracks. The recipe has obviously been updated. The wheat cracker is a nice alternative to the every-day-over-processed variety. It's always good to know how to make from scratch what you like.

- 2 sticks butter
- 1 pound cheddar cheese, grated
- 1 package onion soup mix
- 2 cups flour

Let the butter and cheese come to room temperature, then mix thoroughly. Mix dry ingredients together and add to cheese mix. This may take getting your hands into it to get all of the dry stuff moistened. Shape into two or three rolls, one inch in diameter. Wrap in waxed paper and chill.

Heat oven to 375°. Slice each roll into ¼" thick pieces. Bake on ungreased baking sheet 10-12 minutes or until slightly browned on edges. Makes 14-16 dozen.

WHEAT CRACKERS

THE MIX:

- 3 cups flour
- 2 cups whole wheat pastry flour
- 1 ½ tsp. salt

Blend these three ingredients very well. Measure into three equal portions of one and two-thirds cups of the mix into three zipper-type bags. Label and keep in the freezer.

THE CRACKER:

- 1 'package' of wheat mix
- 1 stick of butter, cold, grated
- 2 large eggs
- 1 T. water

Place mix in a large bowl, add butter and mix well with pastry blender or hand mixer. Scramble eggs and water together, add to wheat/butter mix, and blend again. Dough will be stiff. Make a 2" diameter roll, wrap in waxed paper, and chill for 4 hours.

Heat oven to 375°. Slice dough 1/8" thick. Bake on ungreased baking sheet for 12-15 minutes or until golden brown.

Option: salt before baking.

GRAHAM CRACKERS

I've seen different versions of graham crackers with the simplest being from an 1886 suffragette cookbook that said to 'mix one part cream to four parts milk, add flour'. This is my favorite.

THE MIX: (makes three batches)

- 6 cups whole whMix together very well and divide into three two-cup portions. Place in clean containers that seal well, or zipper-type bags, label, and freeze.

THE CRACKERS: (makes about 48)

- 1 batch cracker mix (2 cups)
- 1 stick of butter
- ¼ cup honey or maple syrup (for a deeper taste, add 1 t. molasses)
- ¼ cup milk

Place mix in a bowl. Cut butter into mix until crumbly. Add milk and honey to form a dough. Divide into four pieces. Roll out to 1/8" thick on a floured surface, smoothing the edges. Cut into rectangles, and prick all over with a fork.

Heat oven to 375°. Bake on a lightly greased cookie sheet, 12-15 minutes until golden.

For a wonderful taste, sprinkle with some cinnamon sugar before baking.

SODA CRACKERS

This is one of my favorites because it's so versatile.

- 6 cups flour
- 1 tsp. salt
- 1 tsp. baking powder
- 1 tsp. baking soda
- 1 cup solid shortening
- 1 cup milk
- Salt

Mix dry ingredients together, cut in shortening. Add milk to form the dough. Roll out thin on a floured surface, smoothing the edges. Cut into squares and prick with a fork. Salt if desired. Heat the oven to 350°. Bake on an ungreased sheet for 10-12 minutes and watch carefully, they burn easily.

** Dry canning crackers is easy if you follow certain rules. The jars and seals must be one hundred percent dry, and the jar edge free of any crumbs. Put crackers in wide mouth jars, fix the seals and rings, and put into a cold oven. Turn the heat on to 250° for 3 hours, and then let cool in the oven. It's that simple.*

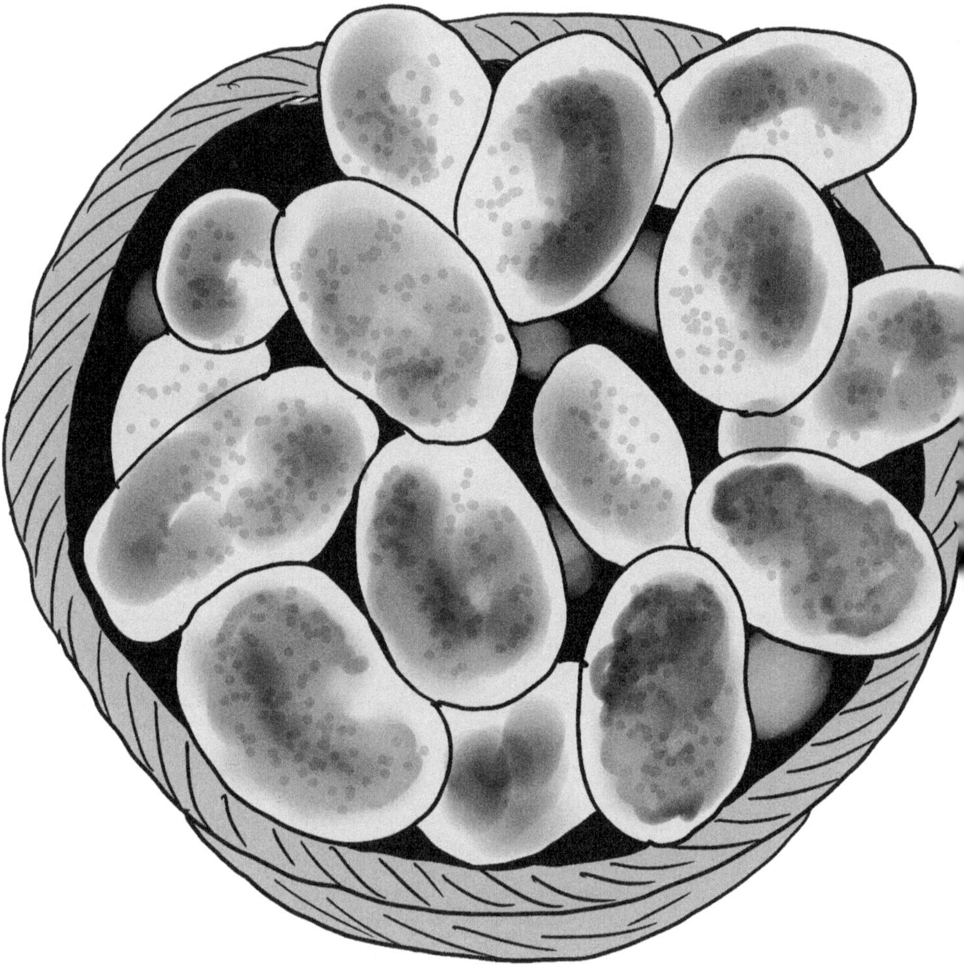

PLANNING AHEAD

Winters here in the Upper Peninsula of Michigan are long and snowy. The snow totals are extreme, with an average of over twenty feet per winter. I make sure that we have enough supplies in November to last until May. Granted, there are a few things I need to bring in, like fresh greens, but basically I have everything we need. Most of what I keep on hand will last a lot longer than six months. Necessity is how I got started on my intensive food storage plan.

I didn't know what to store, so I guessed the first year, and then I took an inventory on November 1. Afterwards, I kept track of everything that was added to the supplies, I then took a second inventory on May 1. That gave me a pretty good idea of what we used over a six-month period. I dated everything with just the month and year. I keep a heavy marker on the shelf closest to where I unload groceries. It takes a few extra minutes to date those twelve cans of evaporated milk, but I know which ones to use first. I can see at a glance what is and isn't being used and what to rotate.

I allocated storage areas for both food and other necessities. Mine is 250 square feet in the basement. I have twelve shelf units, six feet high with five shelves each. Shelves can be removed to provide space for larger items. I also use thin wooden separators to make it easier and more stable for storage of glass canning jars. The very top shelves are used for storing seldom-used items such as canning kettles, food presses, the manual apple corer and cherry pitter, empty jars, blankets, and seasonal clothing.

It made sense to keep the vegetables in one spot, fruits and jams together, with meat and soups in their own place. This also makes taking inventory much easier. It rarely takes more than half an hour to complete either the spring or fall inventories. It's really wonderful to have so much room to organize.

Everyone knows what they like and what they want to have on hand, but I had a need for deeper thinking. Knowing we may not get out of the woods for weeks at a time has really helped me realize what is most important for our food storage. I have a penchant for Caesar salads, so I purchase one tube of anchovy paste per month. We both like turkey, so I buy several when it is on sale and spend the next three days cooking and canning meat and broth.

I store flour in a mouse-proof galvanized trash can, double-lined with heavy trash bags. Even though the basement tends to be damp, there's never been a moisture or bug problem with the food. I store sugar, rice, salt, pasta, dry beans, brown rice, and powdered milk in five-gallon buckets with airtight seals. I found an old wicker laundry basket at a yard sale that was perfect for my harvest of potatoes.

One year I tried storing carrots packed in sand in a buried trash can. Disaster! It gets so cold here that they froze solid. I sure had a mess to clean up the next spring.

SOFT PRETZELS

These make a great unusual snack for casual parties and small gatherings. I first made these when my sons were very small. They loved them plain and I loved them dipped in mustard.

- 2 cups warm water
- 1 T. yeast or 2 packs
- ½ cups sugar
- 2 tsp. salt
- ¼ cup softened butter (1/2 stick)

WASH:

- 1 egg yolk
- 2 T. water
- Coarse sea salt

Mix all the ingredients together (except for the wash), knead, and then put in a bowl with a tight cover. Refrigerate at least 4 hours or overnight.

Divide the dough in half. Make sixteen balls out of each half. Roll the ball out into a six to eight inch rope and twist into a pretzel shape. Place on a greased baking sheet, repeat. Rise until double, at least 30 minutes.

Mix egg yolk and water, brush onto the pretzels, sprinkle with salt.

Bake at 400° for 15 minutes. Cool on wire racks.

Makes 32 pretzels.

NORI ROLLS

Nori rolls are what we recognize as sushi: flavored rice rolled up in a sheet of dried seaweed called Nori. Sushi is not raw fish, although it can be. It's also cooked seafood and it's also vegetables. It's the rice that makes the sushi. Whatever you fill the rolls with it can be topped with thin slivers of Gravlax.

THE RICE:

- 1 cup long grain white rice
- 2 cup water
- ¼ cup rice vinegar
- 2 tsp. salt
- ¼ cup Mirin, sake or dry sherry
- 2 T. sugar or honey
- 6 Nori sheets

FILLINGS:

- Thinly sliced cucumbers, sliced into sticks
- Thinly sliced carrots or celery, blanched and cooled
- Mashed avocadoes
- Cooked shrimp, chopped
- Pickled ginger, sliced

Rinse the rice several times in a colander. Add rice to the water and bring to a boil. Reduce heat and simmer until rice is tender and water is gone. If the rice is still hard, add a bit more water. In another pan, mix vinegar, salt, Mirin, and sugar; heat until sugar is dissolved. Put the cooked rice in a cool bowl, pour vinegar solution over and stir. This is the important part: *stir constantly until cooled.* Fanning helps and a wooden paddle is good to use. The rice will be sweet and sticky. Divide the rice into six portions (it can be left in the bowl).

Lay a Nori sheet on a towel and spread a portion of rice evenly, leaving the edge furthest away clean. I use my fingers to spread the rice evenly. Lay a few pieces of filling in a line closest to you, then start on that end and roll gently, lifting with the towel toward the end with no rice. Cut each roll into six pieces.

DIPPING SAUCE:

- 1 T. grated ginger root
- 1 tsp. wasabi paste
- ¼ cup soy sauce
- green onion, finely chopped

Mix together and let the flavor blend while making the rolls. Soy sauce alone can be used, too. A piece of pickled ginger across the top tastes wonderful, or some finely sliced gravlax.

There are a number of commercial sauces that are equally as good, like duck sauce or fish sauce. There are no rules for dipping.

TORTILLAS & FISH SPREAD

This has endless variations, depending on the fish you use and optional additional fillings.

FISH SPREAD:

- 1 can of salmon or 2 jars canned fish from storage
- 1/3 cup mayonnaise (to taste)
- ½ tsp. Worcestershire sauce
- ½ tsp. liquid smoke
- 1 small onion, finely diced

Open and drain the fish. If using salmon, remove bones and skin. Mash the chunks in a medium bowl with a fork. Add the mayonnaise, Worcestershire sauce, and liquid smoke. Stir until blended and add one small onion, finely chopped. Blend well. The mixture should be wet but not sloppy. If it's not wet enough to hold together, add more mayonnaise, a little at a time.

Divide the mixture into six portions, and spread it evenly on six tortillas, rolling each one tightly. Slice the rolls an inch thick, forming pinwheels, and place on a platter.

Options: Before rolling, sprinkle with dill, lay chives at random, or finely diced celery.

TORTILLAS:

- 4 cup flour
- 1 T. salt
- ¼ pound butter (one stick)
- 1 1/3 cup tepid water

Put the flour and salt in a large bowl. Stir. Cut the butter in with a hand mixer until the bits are small. With the mixer running, add the water all at once and turn on high, blending until everything is moistened, just a few seconds. Scrape the dough off the beaters. Using floured hands, measure out twelve balls, approximately two ounces each (about the size of a large egg). Set each on a floured towel as you form them. Cover with another cloth and let rest 20 minutes. Set a griddle on the stove to heat.

THE RESTING IS IMPORTANT! *If you handle the dough too much, it will toughen and won't roll, but will recover if you let it rest.*

Roll one tortilla out on a floured board and set it on the griddle. Start rolling out another. Turn the first one over, it should have started forming bubbles and might have a golden color in spots. The total cooking time will be 2-3 minutes or less, depending on how hot your griddle is, and on my wood cookstove that can be an iffy thing! Be careful not to let them burn. Move first tortilla to a wire rack, place second one on griddle, roll out a third one, repeat. You will find your rhythm. The tortillas should be soft and pliable.

SPECIAL MOMENTS...

FAWNS

One day as I rounded a curve, a large doe stood in the middle of the road, defiantly not moving. I stopped well away from her and waited for her to move, but she would look back to the side she had come from, then back at me. I soon discovered the reason why when a wobbly legged fawn came out from the bushes. It was very small, and couldn't have been more than a day or two old. It wobbled over to the doe, and they both headed off into the woods. Precious.

My last year in the woods, I rounded another curve, on another road, only to be stopped by another doe in the road... but this one was nursing a fawn. In the middle of the road! I saw a car approaching me, so I flashed my lights. The driver slowed and waited patiently too. I glanced in my rearview mirror and was surprised to see two more cars behind me, all sitting idle while we took in this spectacular insight. It was one of those moments I wish I had a camera with me (that happens a lot!), especially when I saw that the person behind me was leaning out, snapping pictures of this incredible sight. We all sat there patiently for a full 15 fifteen minutes. When we could continue, I inched closer, very slowly. The doe took a few steps and stopped. I inched a bit closer, and she moved to the shoulder, jumping the berm. The fawn tried to follow, but was so small it couldn't climb. It ran toward me several feet, trying to climb in a near panic state, until it reached an area it could maneuver, and then it was gone from sight.

* * *

BABA GHANOUJ (*Ba-Ba-Ga-Nush*)

It sounds strange, but it is one of the delightful ways to eat pita bread. Along with hummus, which is more commonly known, Baba Ghanouj is a great appetizer, snack, or low cholesterol stuffing for deviled eggs.

- 1 large eggplant
- 2 cloves garlic (1 tsp. crushed)
- 1 tsp. coarse salt
- ¼ cup Tahini (sesame seed paste)
- 3-4 tsp. fresh lemon juice
- Fresh parsley
- Olive oil

Prick the eggplant with a fork, wrap in foil, and bake until tender. Let cool in the foil. Scrape the fruit from the skin into a bowl and mash coarsely. Add the garlic and salt, set aside. Mix the Tahini with the lemon juice, and then add to the eggplant, stirring gently, but thoroughly. Spread on a dinner plate, sprinkle with fresh chopped parsley (NOT dried!), and dribble olive oil over all. Wrap in clear plastic wrap and chill.

Serve with triangles of pita bread to scoop.

HUMMUS:
This is very similar to Baba Ghanouj, only substitute the eggplant with a can of chickpeas, also called garbanzo beans.

In a blender, add the chickpeas, juice and all, the lemon juice, and garlic. Blend into a paste. Add the Tahini and salt, along with a pinch of cumin, around ¼ teaspoon. Blend until smooth.

Serve in a bowl, dusted with fresh parsley, and a bowl of pita triangles.

Both of these dishes make an excellent filling for hard cooked eggs, or as vegetarian snack or meal.

THE ICE BOX

When I was planning my move to the UP, I knew I was going to need to make some major adjustments. Yes, I was prepared, even anxious, to learn how to cook on a woodstove; no more quick and easy gas ranges. However, that left me with another dilemma – refrigeration. Since the solar battery system wasn't big enough to handle a refrigerator, and we didn't want the utility bill of gas, I figured an icebox was the answer. I mean, if it was good enough for gramma, it'd be good enough for me. Things changed and progressed from there.

Before I left Lower Michigan, I started searching for an old fashioned icebox. My thoughts were that up here they might be in use and not as available. I soon discovered I was wrong; most camps have gas refrigerators, but I didn't know that then. The few I found were too small. I saw an ad in the local paper from an antique hunter. I called and gave him my price range and requirements. His guarantee was there was no obligation to buy if I didn't like what he found. Three weeks later he called, and I went to his house to take a look. He had found a 'commercial' size, four door, solid oak ice box. It measured 37" wide × 23" deep × 53" high. Interior space is 10.8 cu. feet, big by 1900 standards. It was beautiful! It even still had the brass plate on the front that identified it as a "B.A. Stevens - Manufacturer - Toledo, O". Cool. The shelves were intact and no damage. He pointed out that one door had been repaired, which brought down the antique value. I didn't care; I wanted it for the functionality. I bought it without hesitation. $550. It was a beautiful piece of furniture regardless of a repaired door or cost.

Once it was at the house in the woods, however, and in use, I realized how inefficient the old ice boxes really were. No wonder there was daily ice delivery! Even with it sitting in the very cool basement, I was buying ice every two days, and things were just barely cool. Something needed to be done.

The icebox sat in the basement the several months while the kitchen was completed, but even when ready, we realized the icebox was too heavy for the two of us to move it up the stairs. We *are* talking oak here. Come November and the first good snowfall, we pushed and shoved until we got the icebox back to the walkout basement door. We pivoted it until we got it close to the toboggan we set in place, tipped it carefully on its side, and into the sled. Whew! Once on the toboggan, we pushed and tugged and slid it uphill around the back of the house, then around the end to the front where the porch was closest to the ground, just a step up. Standing it back up, we laid out moving blankets, not wanting to damage the ice box or the decking on the porch. And once again, we tipped it on its side up onto the waiting padding. Once safely on the moving blankets, we pushed and dragged it forty feet into the house! It was comical, but we did the job. It got moved only once after that, and that was to do the flooring.

At the risk of destroying any remaining antique value, I gutted it. The interior was lined with tin to reflect and hold the cold, with absolutely no insulation at all. That's it, but that was typical for back then. Out came the shelves, out came the tin lining. To the sides, ceiling and floor, I put in 2" thick Styrofoam insulation board, and 1½" in the doors. Over that, I fitted shower paneling, making a very washable surface, and screwed it in place. I found snap together plastic coated shelves and added three plastic drawers stacked on the side. Everything fit perfectly. I still put the ice on the top shelf, but the interior was basically all open. One block of ice frozen in a dishpan, rotated before it melted, kept the icebox at 45-50 degrees. It was easy during the winter to just put a dishpan of water on the porch, let it freeze solid, usually overnight, and switch the pans every morning. It became part of my routine. Problem solved, sort of.

During the really, really cold months (below zero), about six weeks in January and February, I would make ice. Lots of it. We ordered 1000 heavy duty bread bags that I would fill with water from the tap, twist tie, and set into a plastic flowerpot out on the porch. I would set up a dozen of these. It would freeze enough overnight to remove the block from the flowerpot form and I would start over. The frozen bag would sit on the porch to finish freezing solid. When there were three dozen or so, I would load up my sled and take them to the sawdust filled icehouse.

During April and May when the temperatures warm up to above freezing, and again in October and early November as they start to decline, I put the perishables in a second 'icebox' that sat on the back porch. My son constructed it much like the antique one, but without the insulation. I figured, why try to keep things 45° *in*side, when it's 45° *out*side? Plus, having the outside icebox let me keep some things frozen in the winter, and away from the critters.

One May, when most of the stuff was locked in the outside box, we left for the weekend on a much needed entertainment trip, returning to discover that a bear had *eaten* my box of wine that I had left on top of the cooler! That bear came back often.

SALADS

PASTA SALAD

This is one of the simplest and most versatile cold salads I make. I have literally added anything I had left over in the refrigerator.

One thing I'd like to point out is that you eat with your eyes first. Food should look good. The various colors in this dish make it very appealing. The taste will demand seconds.

- 1 pound pasta (shells, radiatore, penne, spirals, bowtie – whatever is available or any combination)
- Green onions, radish, sweet peppers (red, yellow, orange or green – or all of them), celery, black olives, all coarsely chopped
- Broccoli, cauliflower, blanched – cut into small flowerets
- 1 bottle of Italian dressing or the Greek dressing, page 59

Cook the pasta to al dente; it should not be too soft to start since it will absorb some of the moisture from the dressing and soften some that way. Drain pasta and rinse several times with cold water, and then drain well. Put it in a large bowl and add dressing. Start with one half the bottle – you can always add more but you can't take it out. Toss well. Add the raw vegetables, saving some to garnish the top.

The broccoli and cauliflower are better when blanched in boiling water one minute; drain and rinse in cold water to stop the cooking process. The green of the broccoli will be much more vibrant and colorful. Toss well. Garnish with a few broccoli flowerets and slivers of red sweet pepper. Chill well. This will keep several days.

THREE BEAN SALAD

This is another quick and easy side dish that can be made ahead of time. Be sure to save the juice from the beans for soup.

- 1 jar home canned green beans, drained
- 1 jar home canned wax/yellow beans, drained
- 1 can kidney beans, drained and rinsed
- 1 medium onion, thinly sliced and cut in half
- Italian dressing to taste

Place all ingredients in a covered bowl and add dressing. Toss well. Chill.

SUBSTITUTIONS: *Regular canned beans can be used, or fresh beans, cooked and cooled.*

CANNED COLESLAW

While this isn't exactly the same as fresh coleslaw, (nothing beats fresh), it's a very good substitute on a cold winter night when the winds are howling. I got this from my friend David, the canning guru on my internet women's group. While cabbage lasts a long time in storage, it doesn't last forever and this is an excellent way to preserve what you've grown.

- 1 medium head of cabbage
- 1 large carrot, optional
- 1 green, red or yellow pepper (or all of them)
- 1 medium onion
- 1 tsp. salt

SYRUP:

- 2 cups ACV (apple cider vinegar)
- ½ cup water
- 2 cups sugar
- 2 tsp. celery seeds
- 2 tsp. mustard seeds

Shred together the vegetables. Add the salt. Let stand 1 hour. Drain the water, then rinse and drain again, twice.

Boil the syrup ingredients together for one minute, cool. Add syrup to vegetables and mix well. I prefer to pack into pint jars. You can always use two jars if having company. Process jars in a boiling water bath for 15 minutes. This slaw may be drained before use and mayonnaise added or used as is. I like to give it a quick rinse, too.

SYRIAN SALAD

A friend of mine who married a man from the Middle-East learned to make this her husband's sister. It quickly became one of my personal favorites.

- 1 head Romaine lettuce, torn
  (see Caesar Salad, page 63 for suggestions on how to crisp lettuce)
- 4 tomatoes, chopped
- 2 cucumbers, peeled, seeded and chopped
- 2-4 green onions, chopped, greens included
- 4 marinated artichoke hearts, chopped

DRESSING:

- 3 whole garlic cloves
- ¼ tsp. coarse salt
- 6 T. fresh lemon juice (2 or 3 whole lemons)
- 3 T. olive oil
- 4 T. Fresh spearmint leaves, chopped, (or 4 T. dried spearmint, crushed not powdered)

In a large salad bowl, mash garlic with the salt. I use a pestle but the bottom of a glass works well too. Squeeze lemons and measure juice. If there are six tablespoons of juice, add three tablespoons of oil; if eight tablespoons, add four of oil. Add lemon juice and oil to bowl, add a large pinch of the mint. Add one half of the tomatoes, cucumbers, and green onions. Layer the lettuce and one half of the remaining mint. Repeat the lettuce layering, then add the rest of the tomatoes, cucumbers, onions, and artichoke hearts. Cover with wet cloth towel to keep from drying, and chill until ready. To serve, toss thoroughly.

TABBOULEH

I've had many versions of this healthy salad. Some have used too much lemon or not enough parsley. Perhaps I feel that way because I had this version first, from a Lebanese family. This can be served with pita bread or by itself. I like stuffing the Tabouli in the pita for a healthy sandwich.

- 2 cups bulgur
- 2 cucumbers, peeled, seeded, diced
- 3 tomatoes, diced
- 1 bunch green onions, cleaned, chopped, greens included
- 2 bunches parsley, finely chopped
- 1/3 cup dried spearmint, crushed not powdered, (I prefer fresh spearmint, chopped)
- Pinch of cumin
- Salt and pepper to taste
- 1 cup olive oil
- 4 lemons, juiced

Soak the bulgur in four cups warm water for 15 minutes. Drain and squeeze the water out, set in a large bowl. Add parsley and toss (if using fresh mint, add now). Mix cumin with dried mint, salt and pepper, sprinkle over parsley and toss. Add cucumbers, tomatoes, and green onions. Pour olive oil and lemon juice over all and toss.

Serve with wedges of warm pita bread for scooping.

ANTIPASTO SALAD

An impressive dish to look at with its variety of colors, it can be a meal by itself.

- 1 head Romaine lettuce, torn into bite sized pieces
- ¼ lb. hard salami, cut into quarters
- Spiced beets cut into quarters
- Red onion, thinly sliced and separated
- Black olives
- Kalamata olives
- Fresh mozzarella cheese balls, cut in half
- Feta cheese, crumbled
- Cherry tomatoes cut in half
- Hot banana pepper rings

GREEK DRESSING:

- 1 cup olive oil
- 1¼ cup red wine vinegar
- 2 cloves garlic, pressed or finely minced (1 T.)
- 2 tsp. *each* onion powder, sea salt, fresh ground black pepper
- 1 T. *each* dried oregano, basil
- 1/8 tsp. fresh ground yellow mustard seed

Place all ingredients into a quart canning jar and shake.

On a platter, spread the lettuce. Ring the lettuce with salami and spiced beets. Arrange the rest randomly, placing the red onions and the feta cheese on the top. Pour one half the dressing over all and serve. Remember, eye appeal!

NAPA CABBAGE SALAD

This is a sweet and sour salad that's crunchy, very tasty, and a snap to make. If you have any left over, understand the noodles lose their crunch in the dressing overnight. We rarely have any leftover!

- 1 medium head Napa Cabbage, thinly sliced and chopped in half
- 1 medium onion, thinly sliced
- 4 ribs celery, thinly sliced
- ½ stick butter
- 1 package Ramen noodles, crushed (reserve the seasoning packet for another use)
- ½ cup sliced almonds
- 2 T. sesame seeds

Sauté noodles, almonds, and sesame seeds in the butter until lightly browned. Set aside. Combine cabbage, onion, and celery and toss. Add noodle mixture on top. Add dressing just before serving.

DRESSING:

- ¼ cup sugar
- ¼ cup vinegar (preferably red or white wine vinegar, but apple cider vinegar will do)
- ½ cup olive oil

Place in a jar and shake to blend.

HENRY THE CHIPMUNK

Of all my woodland friends, furred and feathered, my very favorite was Henry the Chipmunk.

One warm summer day as I sat in a chair on the porch, reading (one of my favorite things to do), I heard this quiet bump, bump, bump, across the porch decking. Mindful to not make any sudden movements, I darted my eyes in that direction. Here came a chipmunk. It nosed around near my feet, around the chair, by the steps, then sat off to the side to groom. After a short while, he left, and I had an idea. Since it seemed he wasn't afraid of me,

I wondered if I could get him closer. I went inside and filled my pocket with some of the sunflower seeds I fed to the birds, and left him a small offering where he had been sitting to groom. Within five minutes he was back, and quickly packed his pouches with the seed, and left again, so I put some more down. We did this several times when I ran out of seeds in my pocket. His next trip to the porch, he nosed around and, not finding any offerings, looked over at me and climbed up on my foot! I got more seeds and put them in my pocket, and he actually climbed into my pocket for his treats! I had a new friend.

Over the course of the next few days, I would sit waiting for Henry to arrive. By that time, I had filled a pint canning jar with seeds so I wouldn't run out, and like I shook the scoop of corn to signal Sara the deer, I would shake the jar to attract Henry's attention. I sometimes think he waited nearby for me, as he would be by my side within moments, looking for his usual handout. It took less than a week to get Henry to sit in my hand to collect his seeds, and he never flinched when I stroked his soft fur, very gently with one finger. Eventually, Henry would sit on my shoulder to groom, or on my lap, or on my book. Sometimes I would just leave the jar open by my side, and he would climb in, fill his pouches, and hop back out. I usually left the jar sitting outside by the door, for my convenience, with the lid on of course. More than once, I could hear the jar being rolled around on the porch, Henry trying to get to the seeds inside.

I did notice other chippies showing up for seeds, but none with Henry's distinctive scar on his left hindquarter. They all ended up with quite a winter food stash somewhere!

One afternoon, Muffin the Cat sat with me, her sunning, me reading, when Henry showed up. He stopped short and very cautiously crept forward, checking out this new addition to our ritual. Oblivious as usual, Muffin paid no attention to this little critter, and Henry, obviously feeling no threat, hopped over her tail, to get to the jar of sunflower seeds.

With that scar as a name tag, I knew it was Henry that showed up year after year. For four years I watched him actually grow grayer and grayer, until one spring, he didn't come back. Animals age just like we do, and like us, they leave this Earthly plane.

CAESAR SALAD

I was surprised when I found out that my all-time favorite, Caesar Salad, did not originate with the Roman Caesar we are all familiar with. A gentleman named Caesar Cardini had a restaurant in Tijuana, Mexico back in the 1920s. It was a popular place to visit during the Prohibition Era in the United States. Mr. Cardini would prepare the salad himself, tableside. Starting with ultra-pure olive oil, he would 'roll' the hearts of romaine to coat them. Garlic, fresh squeezed lemon juice, and Worcestershire sauce were added and again, 'rolled' into the salad. The last was the egg, broken onto the salad, and once more 'rolled'. Whew! I like my way. Also, there were no anchovies in Mr. Cardini's salad. The idea came about, supposedly, from the fact that there are anchovies in Worcestershire sauce … or is it Worcestershire in the anchovy?

For clean, crispy lettuce, separate the leaves, removing any browned edges or veins. Rinse thoroughly. Gently shake the water off and place on a dish towel, spreading the leaves evenly at an angle. Fold the bottom up, one corner in, and then gently roll from that corner. Pull the top corner down, and place the bundle in a large zipper type bag, squeezing the air out before closing. Keep chilled. By squeezing the air out of the bag, the towel is forced into contact with the wet leaves, blotting them dry. Your lettuce will be dry and crunchy.

- 1 tsp. crushed garlic (2 cloves)
- 2 tsp. anchovy paste
- 1 tsp. Worcestershire sauce
- ½ tsp. dry mustard (optional)
- 3 T. lemon juice
- 1 egg yolk
- 1/3 cup olive oil
- 1 T. grated Parmesan cheese
- ½ cup fresh shredded Parmesan or Asiago cheese
- Croutons (optional)

In a large salad bowl, add garlic, anchovy paste, Worcestershire, mustard, and lemon juice. Stir until well blended. Add the egg yolk, stirring gently. Slowly add the olive oil. Do not whisk!! Stir in grated cheese. Add the Romaine, torn into bite sized pieces. Toss thoroughly. Top with croutons. Serve with shredded cheese and fresh ground pepper. Because of the raw egg, this does NOT keep overnight.

LAYERED SALAD

I'm a believer in presentation. If something looks good it's going to taste better. Using a clear glass bowl makes this salad very eye appealing as the layers really stand out. Years ago I entered a seed company contest, using the then-new colored Swiss chard, which I used in this recipe. I was delighted to win an honorable mention.

In a bowl, layer in order:

- 4 cups torn lettuce
  (options: shredded cabbage, spinach, chard or other greens)
- 1 cup sweet pepper, chopped
  (a mixture of colored peppers looks great)
- 1 cup celery, chopped
- 1 cup cooked fresh green peas (or frozen)
- 6 green onions, chopped, greens included
- 1 can sliced water chestnuts
  (or one cup raw, Jerusalem artichokes, scrubbed, diced)
- Shredded Parmesan cheese
- 6 slices bacon, crisply cooked and diced
- Sprinkle the salad with cheese and a few grindings of fresh black pepper.

DRESSING:
Mix 2 cups mayonnaise (or salad dressing) with ¼ cup additional cheese. For a healthier dressing, replace 1 cup of the mayo with sour cream or 1 cup plain yogurt. Spread this mixture evenly over the salad (may be thinned if needed with a few tablespoons of milk or water). Dust with additional cheese, the bacon and maybe some chopped chives for color. Chill. Do not toss, just scoop out.

ADDITIONAL OPTIONS: *If using the brightly colored Swiss chard, use the stems too. Remove stems, chop and blanch quickly to preserve the color.*

EVERLASTING COLESLAW

This really will last four weeks in the refrigerator, or so the claim goes. It's so tasty, though, I've never had it last more than a week.

- 1 large head of cabbage, shredded
- 1-2 large onions, cut in half, thinly sliced
- ¾ cup sugar
- 1 cup white vinegar
- 2 T. additional sugar
- 1 tsp. salt
- 1 tsp. celery seed
- 1 tsp. dry mustard
- ½ cup olive oil

In a large, covered bowl, layer shredded cabbage and onions. Pour the sugar over all and set aside. Combine remaining ingredients in a saucepan and heat to boiling. Pour over the cabbage. Let set for at least 4 hours then toss.

CUCUMBER AND WASABI DRESSING

I was skeptical when I first tried this on a chicken wrap at a restaurant, but was sold with one bite. It's fresh and tangy and can be used many ways. Thinned some, it makes a great salad dressing. Left thick, it's an excellent dipping sauce for vegetables or spread on your sandwich. With the fresh cucumber it doesn't keep for more than a week, so I don't recommend doubling the recipe. What I do recommend is trying the different "carriers" and decide which one you like best.

- 1 cup plain yogurt, sour cream, mayonnaise, or any combination (yogurt will be thinner and healthier)
- 1 cup finely chopped cucumber (peel and seed if using a regular cucumber, whole if using the long, acidless English cukes)
- 1 T. Wasabi, to taste

Put the cucumber in a blender and puree. Add the yogurt and blend. Add the wasabi and blend. Taste and add more wasabi if desired.

CORN SALAD

A friend of mine made something similar to this and I really enjoyed the taste, but I'm not overly fond of avocados, besides, in a disaster situation those will be impossible to get up here, and I wanted something I could make from storage. Plus a word about pasta. Pasta is pasta, with rare exception. If the time comes when you don't have orzo on the shelf, you can use small shells, macaroni, cut up spaghetti, linguini, fettucine, even egg noodles, any pasta will do; I just happen to like the presentation of orzo.

- 2 cups corn (one pint home canned)
- ½ cup orzo pasta
- 2-4 T. cilantro
- 2 limes, juiced or 1/3 cup bottled lime juice
- 1 T. olive oil
- Cherry tomatoes, sliced in half
- 1 green onion, thinly sliced, optional

Cook orzo, 6-7 minutes in boiling salted water, uncovered. Drain and rinse in cold water. Place orzo in a bowl with a lid and stir in the olive oil. Drain the corn and add to the bowl. Add the lime juice, cilantro, tomatoes and green onion. Blend and chill.

OPTIONS: *sliced black olives, diced green, red or yellow sweet pepper, peapods thinly sliced, peas.*

ASIAN SALAD

A delightful change from the usual tossed salad.

- 2 T. peanut oil
- 1 T. soy sauce
- 2 T. rice vinegar
- 1-2 T. cilantro, chopped

Mix together in a large salad bowl and set aside.

- 1 head Romaine, chopped or torn into pieces
- 1 head Red Leaf lettuce, torn into pieces
- 2-4 Green onions, sliced diagonally
- 2-4 Tomatoes, diced or cherry tomatoes, halved
- 1 cup vegetables, steamed and cut small: broccoli, cauliflower

Add to the salad bowl and toss.

BACK TO WORK...

The first summer in the woods was filled with constant work and massive expenses. The idea behind us moving and living off grid was for both of us to 'retire', but the money was quickly running out and Pete didn't want to tap into his retirement account until absolutely necessary. I was the one with the most lucrative and portable trade: massage therapy. The 'business' is in me, my talent, my knowledge, my skill. So it was decided that it would be me to go back to work to support us.

In our little town, mostly supported by tourism, I opened an office in a room adjacent to the real estate office for two days a week. Some days I would sit for hours, with nothing to do, some days I would have one or two clients walk in. One such day is when I met who ended up being my best friend, Kathy. That office was just for the summer months, though. Come winter, another new friend, Maxine, needed help with her café, and still needing an income, I went to work waiting tables.

Friday afternoons, Saturday all day, and Sunday mornings, I would snowshoe out to the car and go to work for what felt like pennies compared to what I was accustomed to making. I was an educated, trained person, and I had never waited tables before. I was sure it was going to be difficult, and was glad it was going to be short term. It actually turned out to be fun. I got to meet many new people, local people, especially on Sunday, during after church breakfast. One such person worked for a local, exclusive, private resort. That spring she approached me, wondering if I would be willing to go to the resort to do massage for one of the members.

Would I????

After that first visit, another member found out I was willing to venture the distance... and then another and another. Within six weeks I was on a regular schedule. I was back to work, full time, not what I had in mind, but it was bringing in a much needed paycheck. This resort was only opened during the summer months, but paid well enough that I didn't have to go back to waiting tables during the winter.

The resort is breathtaking, and for their privacy, I cannot reveal the name, but it's 30,000 acres of pristine woodlands, with numerous lakes and rivers within the boundaries. All fifty of the privately owned resident cabins have river or Lake Superior frontage and the resort has a guarded gate. It is a very nice, secure, safe place to work. Every May I would wait for the first phone call that signaled the resort being open, and every October I would regretfully leave on the last day. Regretfully, yes, but also thankfully. Massage is hard work, and by October I was tired and ready for the rest.

Working all summer had its definite downside. Pete was not interested in maintaining the vegetable garden, even though he had taken the Master Gardening class with me. All he wanted to do was his stained glass. The garden suffered greatly, and produced poorly. I did get enough to harvest and can for the winter, and I was buying more than I was growing, which was NOT part of the plan. I couldn't do it all though, and I had to choose. Days off were spent helping Pete cut firewood for the winter, or collecting kindling, or canning whatever the garden managed to produce, or, or, or.... By October I was very tired and in need of the rest.

This just wasn't going as planned....

Eighteen years later, I'm still working with the members of that resort. We've grown very fond of each other and they have become my friends, even though our economic status is worlds apart.

PASTAS, BREADS AND PASTRIES

PASTA

FRESH PASTA

This is so simple to make and it will take you a long way.

- 2 cups flour
- 1 tsp. salt
- 1T. oil
- 1 egg
- Water to make 4 oz. with egg and oil

Put the flour and salt in a bowl and stir to blend. Scramble the egg, oil, and water together, then add the flour. Using a dull knife (like a butter knife) start cutting in the flour by dragging the knife back and forth, adding the flour into the wet ingredients. When it gets to be too difficult, start using your hands and squeeze the bits together. When the ball in the center gets too sticky, it's time to add more flour. Do it once, you'll understand.

If you can't get all of the flour into the mixture, don't worry about it. It all depends on the humidity of the day. When you've gotten all you can into the mixture, take that ball and knead it a few more minutes. Leave it in the bowl and cover; let rest* for 30 minutes.

I prefer a marble board for the next step, or at least one you can take to the sink to wash. Put a quarter cup of flour in the center of the board and place the ball of dough on top. Press it down with your hand and then turn it over. Start rolling it out in a circle, turning often to keep both sides coated with flour. I personally prefer a marble rolling pin as well, but use whatever you have. When it won't roll anymore, stop, cover with a towel and let it rest again. Repeat until the pasta is thin. Remember, the pasta will plump when cooked.

Cut to your desired shape and either cook or dry. This raw pasta will cook faster since you're not rehydrating it. Small pieces are nice for soups, longer pieces for gravy or sauces and sheets for lasagna or manicotti.

---

* This resting time is very important to pasta.

EGG AND CHEESE PASTA

This recipe takes a little trust the first time you try it. The heat of the pasta *does* cook the egg. Trust me.

- 1 basic pasta recipe, cut into ribbons
- 2 eggs
- ½ cup grated Parmesan cheese
- 6 strips bacon
- 1 clove garlic, crushed
- ¼ cup dry white wine
- Salt and fresh ground pepper
- ½ cup shredded Parmesan or Asiago cheese

Start water boiling for the pasta. Beat eggs with grated Parmesan or Asiago cheese in serving bowl and set aside. Chop bacon into small pieces and fry until crisp. Add garlic and wine, cook until reduced by half. Keep hot over a very low heat.

Cook pasta in salted boiling water until tender. Drain quickly and add to bacon, stirring to gather up all the tasty little bits. While very hot, add pasta to the egg mixture and toss. Keep covered until ready to serve. Serve with extra cheese.

This makes an excellent side dish for four or a main dish for two, just add a salad.

VARIATIONS: *The bacon can be replaced with ham or pancetta, or left out for a vegetarian dish. Try adding some onion to the cooking bacon!*

PIEROGI

Pierogi are a filled Polish dumpling. The basic dough here is a bit richer than regular pasta and it is rolled very thin. A good sharp 3" biscuit cutter works perfect. I used to use a tuna can with both ends removed, however, on the new cans you can only remove one end. Dip the cutter in flour with each cut and keep the circles as close together as possible. The left over dough is great to dry and use in soup.

DOUGH:

- 3 eggs
- 2 tsp. salt
- ½ cup water
- 3 cups flour

Beat eggs with water. In a bowl, place flour and salt. Make a 'well' in the center of the flour and add the egg mixture. Blend the flour in small amounts at a time with a knife, until the flour is absorbed. Knead slightly to collect all bits of dough and finish blending all particles. Cover and let rest 20 minutes. Divide in half and roll very thin on a floured board, about 1/8" thick. Cut circles.

Place a small spoonful of filling a little to one side on each round. Moisten the edge with water, fold over and seal edges tightly, making a half moon. Drop pierogi into salted boiling water. Cook gently for 3-5 minutes. Do not over crowd. Lift out with a slotted spoon. Place on a clean towel and cook the rest. Melt some butter in a fry pan and fry the dumplings until lightly golden.

SAUERKRAUT AND MUSHROOM FILLING:

- 2 cups sauerkraut, rinsed, drained well and chopped
- 1 small onion, diced
- 1 cup mushrooms, diced
- 2 T. butter

Sauté onion and mushrooms in butter until limp. Add sauerkraut and heat through.

POTATO AND SQUASH FILLING:

- 1 cup mashed potatoes
- 2 small onion, diced
- 1 cup cooked, mashed butternut squash
- 1 T. butter

Sauté onion in butter until limp. Blend everything together, add salt and pepper to taste.

Once boiled and cooled, pierogi can be frozen. Thaw and then fry in butter.

FRITTATA

A frittata as I learned about it, is an egg pie without a crust. There are probably as many recipes and versions of frittatas as there are of chili. This is mine, and it's a good one for cleaning out the refrigerator too. It makes an excellent brunch dish.

If you don't have any pasta left over from dinner the night before then cook some fresh. I feel long pasta, like spaghetti or linguini, gives the best results.

- ¼ lb. pasta, cooked
- 4-6 eggs, scrambled
- ½ cup shredded cheese, your choice
- ½ cup ham, optional
- 6 strips bacon
- ¼ cup each broccoli, cauliflower, onions, bell pepper, peapods, all cut small (or anything you have in the refrigerator)

Cook the bacon in a fry pan. Remove and dice. In the same pan add onions and peppers, cook one minute, add the rest of the vegetables, plus the ham and bacon. Heat thoroughly. Stir in the pasta, heating for one minute. Add the scrambled eggs and stir to coat everything. Reduce heat and cover until eggs are set. Add cheese on top, cover and remove from heat.

To serve, cut into wedges and serve with toast.

CRAB STUFFED ZITI

Ziti are short, round, tubular pasta, an inch or so long. These will be made into an appetizer, but could easily be covered with a light, cheesy cream sauce. When I made these for the first time, I told my son he was a guinea pig for the dish. He replied with a smile, "Ah, memories of my childhood!" Yes, I tried out many new dishes on my family. Makes 36.

- ¼ lb. ziti (36 pieces), cooked al dente, rinsed with cold water, drain well and toss with 1 T. olive oil.

THE CRAB STUFFING:

- 1 6oz. can of crab meat, drained
- ¼ cup seasoned bread crumbs
- 1 tsp. pepper blend #2, page 188
- 1 tsp. Worcestershire sauce
- Dash of liquid smoke
- 4 T. mayonnaise
- 1 T. shallot, finely chopped
- 1 T. celery, finely chopped
- 1 T. milk
- Block cheese, your choice, cut into 36 bite sized pieces
- Pitted Olives, either black, green, or Kalamata

Drain the crab meat, squeezing almost dry. Put in a bowl and separate to flake. Add the bread crumbs and pepper blend. Mix well. Add the mayonnaise, Worcestershire, and liquid smoke. Blend well. If too dry, add the milk.

Now comes the fun part. Using your fingers, take a small bit of crab and stuff into a ziti, being careful not to split the pasta. Stand it up in a storage container that has a lid. Chill until you're ready to assemble.

To assemble, thread one ziti onto a toothpick, add an olive, and spear onto a chunk of cheese to hold it upright.

THE GARDEN

The garden was approximately fifty feet from the barn, and was cleared to a 150′ × 150′ area. The actual working garden was 100′ × 100′. We cut posts from logs to outline the garden and sunk them deep, leaving the posts approximately 4 feet high. Then we strung several rows of wire that would be electrified by a garden solar charger. The charge sent out a pulse, and for the most part it worked, though not as well as we had hoped. The ground was also very uneven around the edges along the fence line, and I found that those pesky raccoons could get under at certain spots. The wire also was prone to "shorting out" when grass grew too close, touching it, or a branch fell on it. I walked the perimeter every two days, clearing debris. All this didn't happen until the second summer. There was way too much to do first that was more important than gardening, but the garden was never far from my thoughts.

Before I left downstate, I took Master Gardening classes, knowing our own production would eventually be our main food source. At least that was the idea. I had high hopes of fertile ground, but still did the recommended soil sampling in the spring. Of course our spring still meant feet of snow on the ground!

That first soil sample indicated we had very poor soil for growing vegetables. Lots of fertilizer and even more lime was added every year, just to grow a few crops. Watering was the major issue.

Cistern Watering

When I planted that first garden, I was hauling buckets of water from the house with the garden tractor and cart. It was a very slow process. One evening over cocktails, we hit upon a solution: the barn. We built an

8 × 8 platform, ten feet high behind the barn, out of all natural materials. We purchased a 300 gallon cattle watering tank and set it on the platform. Pete then ran gutters along one side of the barn roof that down-spouted into the tank. I almost never ran out of water for the garden after that. I had wanted to attach PVC pipe to the new cistern to get the water flow to the edge of the garden high up, at which point a hose could be attached. Since the garden was slightly uphill from the cistern it made sense to me to keep the water line high for the sake of gravity, however Pete disagreed and I was limited to the hose attached directly to the cistern spigot. The gravity feed was barely acceptable, but better than hauling water from the house. Over the course of the first two years, I saved enough empty plastic bottles to begin my 'drought watering' system. Cutting the bottom out of the two liter bottles, I then buried the bottle, neck down about a third deep, right next to a new plant or in the center of a hill of seeds. By filling the bottle, the water went right to the roots where needed, and wasn't lost on the surface. Much less water was required to keep everything flourishing. I planted plenty of tomatoes, peppers, beets, carrots, cucumbers, squash, both summer and winter, rows and rows of potatoes, and corn. That garden did remarkably well. Then we added strawberries, asparagus, Jerusalem artichokes, and horseradish - stuff that would grow on its own.

I was really delighted with my first crop! I had three bushels of potatoes when I was done drying them on the front porch. They kept remarkably well in wicker baskets on the bottom shelf in the basement pantry. What wasn't eaten by the next summer was replanted. I dried the hominy corn, then hulled it into a wide basket and tossed, letting the wind winnow it, just like days of old. It never ceases to amaze me how good cornbread tastes from home grown, fresh ground corn.

Next to the potatoes in the pantry were the winter squash baskets, filled with acorn, pumpkin, butternut, and spaghetti squashes. Summer squash had long since been canned and the jars lined up like ready soldiers next to the countless jars of tomatoes, beans, greens, carrots, spiced beets, and pickles. I was in heaven. This was my destiny.

BREAD

BASIC BREAD

This is the recipe I have used my entire baking life, and that's a long time. For my first loaf of bread, the milk was whole and rich with cream and I had to scald it to kill the enzymes that would kill the yeast. This process was done first so it could cool to a useable temperature. The milk was brought up in heat to near but not at boiling – that's "scalding". Because it was hot I added the butter to melt and to help bring the temperature down. This step is no longer necessary with all the commercial processing done to milk these days. If we ever go back to *real* milk, this will again be a needed step.

A word about yeast as we get started: *heat kills yeast, freezing does not*. Keeping yeast in the freezer is the best way to keep it fresh and viable. Granulated yeast can go straight from the freezer to the bowl, there is no thawing needed. The yeast *will* die if stored in the refrigerator.

Once you master basic bread, the variations are limited only to your imagination.

The options here are dependent on what you have on hand. If you don't have fresh milk, you can add in powdered milk. If you don't have that, use all water; just keep the *amount* the same. If you don't have butter or margarine, use oil. It's that simple.

- 1 cup warm (not hot) milk
- ½ cup warm water
- 1 T. sugar
- 1 T. dry yeast (or one packet)
- 1 tsp. salt
- ¼ cup oil or (melted/softened) butter
- 3-4 cups flour

In a large bowl, add the water, sugar, and yeast together and stir. After a few minutes the yeast should begin to bubble. This is called 'proving' the yeast, as in proving it's still alive and viable.*

NOTE: *If your liquid is too hot it will kill off the yeast and your bread will not rise. It is better to have your liquid too cool than too hot.*

Once you've 'proven' your yeast is good, add your liquids in and stir, then add the salt and one cup of flour. Stir until blended. Start adding one cup of flour at a time until a stiff dough forms. Scrape the bowl and knead lightly in the bowl to collect all the bits. Turn onto a floured surface and knead, adding flour as needed to keep from sticking to the surface. After kneading 5-8 minutes, add 1 T. oil to the bowl, then add the ball of dough and turn to coat it with the oil. Cover with a clean towel and let it rest for 1 hour. Punch it down, cover with the towel, and let it rise 1 hour or so until double in size.

Turn the dough out onto the lightly floured surface and knead it just enough to get the big bubbles out. Form it into an oval and place in a greased bread pan. Cover and let it rise again until it is an inch or two over the top of the pan. You can also make a round loaf and place the dough on a cooking sheet.

Preheat the oven to 350° while the bread is in the second rise and then bake for approximately 40 minutes. If your oven has hot spots, turn after twenty minutes. When a probe thermometer reads 185°, it's done. Turn the loaf onto a cooling rack. Slice when cooled.

FRENCH BREAD

Years ago we could buy long, crusty loaves of bread at the bakery, wrapped in paper. It makes my mouth water just thinking about them. French bakers are required by law (or so I've read) to use only the ingredients you will find here. Of course, they have more experience and special ovens, but you will be delighted how your bread will come out, and more so, how easy it really is.

- 1 ¼ cup warm water
- 1 T. yeast (one packet)
- 1 ½ tsp. salt
- 3-4 cups white flour
- Cornmeal

Mix water and yeast, stir to dissolve, and wait 5 minutes or until you see some bubbles. I will confess that I often add just a pinch of sugar for the yeast to prove. Add the salt and gradually add flour until you have a soft dough. Knead lightly in the bowl to get all the bits of flour and then turn onto a floured board. Knead for 10 minutes. (This longer kneading time is crucial to a good dough.) Very lightly oil the bowl— just a few drops of olive oil will do— and return dough for its first rise. Cover with a towel and let it rise for 2 hours. Punch down and let rise again for 1 hour.

If using a curved baking pan designed for French bread, sprinkle the pan with some of the cornmeal. Divide the dough in half and roll each half into a piece approximately 12" long and place on top of the corn meal. If using a cookie sheet, divide the dough in three or four pieces 6" long. Cover with the towel and let rise 1 hour.

After the second rise, boil a kettle of water and preheat the oven to 450°. On the lowest rack place an oven proof bowl or pan filled with the boiling water. Slash each loaf twice with a razor and lightly spray with water; place on the center rack. After 5 minutes, spray again; another 5 minutes, another spray. Continue baking until total time is 25 minutes. The spraying with water gives the bread a wonderfully crunchy crust and the water in the pan keeps the humidity high.

Cool slightly, but serve hot. The bread can be reheated by popping back in the oven for a few minutes. If you wrap it in foil, it will soften the crust. Store in a cloth or paper bag.

ITALIAN BREAD

This is similar to the French bread, only with the addition of oil and potato a slightly different texture and taste is achieved. This is a favorite around here. The two smaller loaves are convenient for company, and I like having a standard bread loaf for sandwiches for myself.

- 3 cups warm water
- 3 T. sugar
- 1 T. dry yeast
- 1 T. salt
- ¼ cup olive oil
- ¼ cup dried potato flakes
- 7-8 cup flour
- Sesame seeds, optional
- Egg yolk beaten with 1 T. water, optional

Mix the water with sugar and yeast. Let stand 5 minutes to prove. Stir in the salt, oil, and potato flakes. Start adding the flour, beating well after each addition, until it's hard to stir. Turn out onto a floured board, scraping the bowl. Knead for 10 minutes. This is one of the long ones, obtaining a nice smooth dough. Put a splash of oil in the bowl, then the dough, turning to oil all sides. Cover and let rise 1 hour. Punch down, knead lightly in the bowl, cover and let rise another 1 hour. Punch down again. Divide the dough in half, then divide one piece in half again.

Lightly spray or oil the French bread pan and sprinkle with some sesame seeds. This will be for the two smaller loaves. Prepare a standard loaf pan the same way for the remaining dough. Form the two small loaves into 8" long pieces and place on top of the sesame seeds. Fold the larger piece so it fits in the loaf pan. Cover and let rise 45 minutes. Slash the tops diagonally with a razor and then brush the bread with the beaten egg and liberally sprinkle on more sesame seeds. Bake in a preheated 350° oven for 40 minutes.

RYE BREAD

Ever wonder how the bakery gets that special flavor with rye bread? It took some trial and error, but I've come up with a very acceptable substitution recipe. This calls for only white flour, although you can use whatever combination you're comfortable with: some whole wheat, some rye.

- 1 tsp. anise seed
- 2 tsp. caraway seed
- 1 tsp. fennel seed
- 1 cup boiling water

Bruise anise, caraway and fennel seeds in an herb crusher, or with the bottom of a glass in a shallow bowl. Pour boiling water over the seeds and allow to cool. This is the most important step and can even be done the night before. The seeds are the flavor! By soaking them in boiling water, you are softening them and releasing their flavor into the water. The water will now give a more consistent flavor to the rest of the bread.

- 1 cup warm water
- 2 tsp. yeast
- 1 T. sugar
- ½ cup instant potatoes
- ½ cup instant milk
- 1 tsp. salt
- ¼ cup oil
- Flour

Prove the yeast with the second cup of water, sugar, and yeast. Add molasses if using, instant potatoes, milk, salt, oil, and one cup of flour. Stir until blended. Add seed mixture. Blend well. Gradually add flour until you have a workable dough. Knead on floured surface for 8-10 minutes. Place in oiled bowl, cover, and let rise 1 hour. Knead lightly and form into loaf. Place in oiled loaf pan, cover with a towel and let rise until it's over the edge of the pan by one inch. Bake in a preheated 350° oven for 30-40 minutes, or until it reaches an internal temperature of 185°. Remove from the pan and cool on a wire rack.

VARIATIONS:

You can reduce the amount of the second cup of water to ¾ cup if you use potato water and eliminate the instant potatoes. You can also use leftover mashed potatoes.

For a sweeter bread, use 1 tsp. sugar for proving and 1 T. molasses for flavor, which will also darken the bread.

BURGER BUNS

Having a burger in a bun, whether it's ground beef, venison, or bear, just makes things feel normal in a not-so normal world. I was totally amazed the first time I made these. I haven't bought buns since!

- 3 cup flour
- ¼ cup potato flakes
- 1 T. yeast
- 1 tsp. salt
- 2 T. sugar
- ¼ cup oil
- 1¼ cup warm water
- 2 eggs

Mix water, yeast, and sugar. Let stand 5 minutes. Add salt, oil, and potato flakes, plus ½ cup of flour. The flour gives the egg something to cling to. Add the egg and stir until smooth. Add the flour half cup at a time until stiff. Knead flour in until you have a smooth dough. Return to an oiled bowl, cover with a towel, and let rise 1 hour. Divide in twelve balls, about 2½ ounces each. Place on a floured cloth, cover and let rest 10 minutes. Lightly spray or grease a 12 × 18 pan, and sprinkle with some corn meal. Line the balls up on the pan and flatten each one with the palm of your hand to form a 3" circle and they are almost touching. Cover with the towel and let rise 1 hour or until they are 'crowded'. Bake at 350° for 20 minutes or until golden.

To make hotdog buns, roll each ball until they are about five inches long. Place on baking sheet, close but not touching. Precede as with the burger buns.

While baking, the buns should grow together and get thicker. Slice when cool.

SOURDOUGH BREAD

Sourdough used to be the *only* way breads were made generations ago. The sourdough was perpetuated and kept active by using it and replenishing it constantly. There's a good reason to fall back on the old ways, like when there is no more yeast.

Sourdough can be touchy, and I learned the hard way to *not* use any metal when working with it. So now it's only glass bowls and wooden spoons.

To make a sourdough starter: In a glass bowl or container, add a cup and a half of warm water, a tablespoon of sugar (or honey), a tablespoon of dry yeast, and two cups of flour. Stir it well, drape a dish towel over it, and set it near the cookstove, or some other place to stay warm. The next day stir down the bubbling mixture and set it in the refrigerator for two days to cure/sour.

Take half out. Into the starter canister, add another cup of water and a cup of flour, stir well, and put it back in the refrigerator to ripen. With the reserved half, add two cups of warm water and two cups of flour, stir well, cover. This will sit out overnight to sour and will be ready for use in the morning.

Initially, it's a lot of work and time, but I remember back many years ago when I made sourdough regularly I had a starter sponge ready every morning, it was much easier.

SOURDOUGH ENGLISH MUFFINS

- 1 cup starter: 1 cup warm water/milk, plus 1 cup flour, which we put together last night, remember?
- 2 cup flour
- 1 tsp. salt
- 1 T. baking soda
- 2 T. sugar
- Cornmeal

Mix one cup of flour, salt, baking soda, and sugar together, then add to the starter. Add enough flour to form a workable dough and knead until smooth, adding flour as necessary, about 5 minutes. Cover with a towel and let rest 10 minutes. Roll the dough out to about an inch, cover, and let rest another 10 minutes. Cut with a 3" cookie or biscuit cutter, and place rounds on a piece of wax paper or towel, sprinkled well with cornmeal. Do NOT let the muffins touch. Sprinkle more cornmeal on top and cover. Let rise 1 hour.

Bake on an ungreased preheated griddle for 20-30 minutes, turning several times so they don't burn. Allow to cool before cutting.

SOURDOUGH PANCAKES

Begin with the starter you fixed last night.

- 1 cup flour
- 1 tsp. baking powder
- 1 tsp. salt
- 1 tsp. baking soda
- 2 eggs, beaten
- ½ cup milk
- ¼ cup melted butter

Mix dry ingredients and set aside. Mix eggs, milk, and butter together. Mix the dry ingredients and the milk mixture into the starter, beating until smooth. Cook pancakes on a hot greased griddle, turning once. Enjoy with fresh maple syrup, jam, or fresh fruit.

PIZZA DOUGH

One of the really nice things about this dough is its versatility. Add a few herbs of your choice and obtain a new flavor. Bake it by itself, or with a sprinkle of cheese or garlic salt and it's a great snack. This will make four standard pizzas or two 12 × 18 sheet style.

- 2 cups warm water
- 1 T. yeast
- 1 T. sugar
- ¼ cup oil
- 1 egg
- 4-5 cup flour

Stir together water, sugar, and yeast. Let stand 5 minutes. Add salt, oil, egg, and one cup flour, mix well. Add flour one cup at a time until you have a soft dough and knead in the bowl a few minutes. Cover and let rest 30 minutes. Lightly spray the pans. Divide the dough. Pat out in a circle on the pan. Drizzle oil on the dough, then start pushing the dough with your fingers to the edges. If the dough won't stay where you push it, let it rest a few minutes, then continue. Add the sauce and toppings of your choice and bake in a preheated oven at 400° for 20 minutes or until bottom of the crust is golden.

This also makes wonderful bread sticks! Pat the dough out on the 12 × 18 pan and score, but don't cut, one inch strips 12″ long. Then score again down the middle of the 18″ length, leaving you with six inch sticks. Allow to rise 30 minutes, dust with cheese, and then bake. While still hot, cut along the score marks. Dip into any sauce.

PITA BREAD

This is also called Pocket Bread, Syrian Bread, or Kangaroo Bread. There is no oil used, which is why it dries out quickly. Only make enough for your immediate use. It's simple enough to make every day. The high heat for baking causes the bread to expand quickly, creating that famous pocket.

- 2 ½ cup warm water
- 1 T. Sugar
- 1 T. dry yeast
- ½ tsp. salt
- 6-8 cups flour

Mix water with sugar and yeast. Let stand 5 minutes to prove. Add salt, then flour one cup at a time until you have a stiff dough. Turn on to a floured board and knead in additional flour until no longer sticky, approximately five more minutes. Place in an oiled bowl, cover, and let rise 1 hour. Punch down; knead lightly to get out the big bubbles. Divide into eight balls. Roll each ball out to ¼" thick. If the bread won't roll out easily, allow it to rest a few minutes more. Place on a floured cloth towel. Do not allow to touch each other. Cover with another towel and let rest for 30 minutes to rise.

Preheat the oven to 500°. Using lightly oiled cookie sheets, bake one or two at a time in a very hot oven. Baking should be watched carefully. About 6-8 minutes is all it takes for the bread to brown lightly. Don't be alarmed if the bread doesn't "blow up" in the oven, the pocket can be sliced in when cooled.

This recipe makes eight large or twelve small pitas. Cut the round in half and stuff with anything you desire.

EZEKIEL BREAD

It's been said that Ezekiel bread contains all the nutrients the body needs to survive, and that this was the only food that Ezekiel ate during his journey. *Ezekiel 4:9.* It's tasty, and because there isn't any milk or eggs, it stays fresh a long time. It's a high protein, high fiber batter bread.

King James Bible
Ezekiel 4:9: *Take thou also unto thee wheat, and barley, and beans, and lentiles, and millet, and fitches, and put them in one vessel, and make thee bread thereof, according to the number of the days that thou shalt lie upon thy side, three hundred and ninety days shalt thou eat thereof.*

- 2 1/2 cups hard red wheat
- 1 1/2 cups spelt
- 1/2 cup barley
- 1/4 cup millet
- 1/4 cup lentils
- 2 T. dried Great Northern beans
- 2 T. dried red kidney beans
- 2 T. dried pinto beans

Mix all grains and beans in a large bowl and mill into a fine flour. When grinding something of this nature, it's best to do it in stages. First grind is to crack the beans, next grind is to turn it into meal, and the final grind is to make flour. Depending on your grinder there may be more than three steps.

Measure into a large bowl:

- 4 cups warm water
- 1 cup honey or maple syrup
- 1/2 cup oil
- 2 T. yeast

Mix and set aside for 5 minutes until frothy.

Measure 5 ¼ cups flour and add 2-3 tsp salt. Add to the liquids. Mix with a strong wooden spoon until stretchy and elastic - about 7 minutes.

This is a batter bread that will not form a smooth ball. Pour into three greased bread pans in even amounts.

Place pans in a cold oven on lowest heat to rise (170°). Allow to rise to within 1/2 inch of tops of pans and NO MORE or it will overflow and trash your oven. Mine takes about 15-20 minutes.

Once risen, WITHOUT OPENING THE DOOR, turn the heat up to 350°. If you open the door, the cool air will cause the bread to fall. Bake at 350°, about 25-30 minutes until nicely browned on top. Remember, this is a cake-like bread and will not be like regular yeast breads. You may have to experiment with cooking times. Brush butter on the tops once out of the oven.

CREPES

There are lots of uses for crepes, such as spreading with homemade jam, or rolling up and slicing as a breakfast dessert. This will be used later for the Mid-East Feast at the end of the section on meats.

- ½ cup flour
- ½ tsp. salt
- 4 eggs
- 3 T. melted butter
- 1 cup whole milk

Mix flour with salt. Add eggs and one half cup of milk, beat until smooth. Add the rest of the milk and the butter. Blend well. Let rest, chilled, at least 2 hours.

Preheat flat griddle or a crepe pan. Lightly oil. Over medium heat, use a small soup ladle or a ¼ cup measure, pour batter in center, tipping the pan to spread and make thin. Watch carefully, and as soon as the surface loses the shine (after a few you'll understand) lift from griddle with a spatula and move to a wire rack. If using a crepe pan, the crepe should tip out easily. Do not turn over. The bottom should only be slightly browned. Repeat, stirring the batter each time before dipping. Cool before stacking. May be made ahead. Keep covered with a loose towel.

Makes approximately one dozen.

SAVORY FOCACCIA

This is closer to a true focaccia. It can be sliced and eaten like a pizza or cut into pieces for dipping into a sauce.

- One basic bread recipe, page 83
- Dried Herbs: Basil, oregano, sage, rosemary (fresh or dried), fresh ground pepper, sea salt
- 2 T. Olive oil
- Onions, sliced and cooked, optional
- ¼ cup cheese: Parmesan, Asiago or mozzarella, your choice and optional

Preheat the oven to 400°.

After the second rise of the bread, divide in half and pat out onto two pizza pans. Spread one tablespoon of olive oil on each piece. Sprinkle liberally with the herbs of your choice.

At this point, the focaccia is ready for the oven, however, you can now add the onions and/or the cheese if you choose. Bake for 30 minutes.

FLAT BREAD

This has so many uses it's hard to serve a Mid-Eastern meal without it. This is the basis for meat, spinach, or potato filled pies or Zahtar bread.

Zahtar spice is a combination of savory, thyme, sumac, and sesame seeds and is available in Middle Eastern stores, already mixed to proper balance. It has a wonderfully musty taste. The bread is then eaten plain or dipped in olive oil or yogurt sauce.

THE DOUGH:

- 1 cup warm water
- 1 tsp. dry yeast
- 1 T. sugar
- 3 T. olive oil
- 1 tsp. salt
- 3 cups flour

Mix water, yeast, and sugar, let stand 5 minutes. Add remaining ingredients, the flour a half cup at a time. Knead 5 minutes and let rest 30 minutes in a covered, oiled bowl. Punch down, lightly knead out the bubbles, and divide into eight balls. Using your hands and a bit of oil, pat out into a flat circle ¼" thick. Let rest 15 minutes and then grill on an open fire or grill, one at a time (two if you have the grill space). It should only need a minute or so on each side.

FOR ZAHTAR BREAD:

Preheat oven to 400°.

Mix ½ cup olive oil with ¼ cup Zahtar spice. Pour onto dough, working in with fingers as you push the dough out into a circle. Bake for 15 minutes at 400°.

BAGELS

These are actually fun to make.

- 2 cup warm water
- ¼ cup instant potatoes
- 1 T. dry yeast
- 1 T. sugar
- 1 T. salt
- 1/3 cup oil
- 3 eggs, scrambled
- 6-7 cup flour
- Boiling water plus 1 T. sugar

Mix the water, yeast, and sugar to prove the yeast. After the yeast bubbles, add the instant potatoes, salt, oil, eggs and blend. Add two cups of flour and mix until smooth. Keep adding one cup of flour at a time until it becomes hard to stir. Turn the mix out onto a floured board and knead for 10 minutes, adding additional flour to keep the dough from being sticky. Coat the bowl with a few additional drops of oil and set the dough in, turning to coat. Cover the bowl with a towel and let rise for 1 hour. Punch down and let rest 10 minutes.

Preheat the oven to 450°.

Fill a deep pot with the boiling water and add the sugar. Keep the water boiling.

Divide the dough in half, keeping one of the halves covered. Divide the other half into twelve pieces. Cup your hand over one piece and form into a bun. Set on a lightly floured surface, stick a floured finger into the center and twirl to make a hole. Set aside and make six. Drop bagels into the boiling water two or three at a time, so they are not crowded. When they rise to the top, turn them over and continue to boil another 5 minutes. Remove with a slotted spoon and place on a greased baking sheet. Repeat. Bake for 15 minutes in the oven until golden. Cool on a wire rack. Repeat with the other half of dough.

VARIATIONS:

ONION BAGELS: add one package of dry onion soup mix just before adding the flour.

RAISIN BAGELS: add one tablespoon of cinnamon plus one cup of raisins before adding the flour.

STUFFED FRENCH TOAST

Just thinking about this makes my mouth water. Each of these delights requires two slices of day old bread.

- One 8 ounce container of plain soft spread cream cheese, room temperature
- One lemon, squeezed of juice and zested

Blend the lemon and zest into the cheese. Set aside.

- 4 eggs
- ¼ cup milk
- ½ tsp. vanilla

Scramble together in a bowl or pan that will hold two slices of bread and set aside.

4 thick slices of bread, preferably home made

To assemble, spread a thick layer of the cheese blend on two slices of bread, avoiding the edges. Top with remaining slices. Put the stacked bread in the egg mixture for one minute. Turn over, leaving in the egg to soak until ready to cook, but no longer than 5 minutes. Heat a griddle to hot, add 2 T. butter, melt. Cook the French toast to golden brown, turning once.

To serve, cut the bread into two pieces at angle. Drizzle 1 T. maple syrup on each piece and dust with powdered sugar. Garnish the plate with a piece of fruit, such as a strawberry fan, kiwi or grapes.

OPTIONS: *Instead of lemon, use a lime or half of an orange. For a fruity taste use mashed fresh raspberries, blueberries, or strawberries.*

From storage, use 1 t. extract or 1 T. bottled juice instead of fresh.

Although I don't have a separate section for rice or simple side dishes, I have a few favorite recipes I want to share.

RICE

CHANTERELLE RISOTTO

Risotto is a method of cooking rice. It's time consuming as you will see, but the results are a tender, flavorful dish.

We start with one pound of cleaned Chanterelle mushrooms. This is one of those flexible amounts. Have more? Use more. Have less? That's okay. You can also use a combination of mushrooms.

- 3 cups chicken broth
- 3 T. olive oil
- 1 pound (or more) Chanterelles, thinly sliced (or a blend of mushrooms)
- 1 shallot, diced
- 1 clove garlic, minced
- ¾ cup rice (your choice)
- ½ cup dry white wine
- Salt and fresh ground pepper to taste
- 2 T. butter
- 1/3 cup fresh shredded Parmesan cheese
- Chives or parsley for garnish

Warm the broth in a saucepan. This is essential to a good risotto. Adding cold broth stops the cooking process, so always add warm.

Heat 2 T. Oil in a large sauté pan, add the mushrooms. (Wild mushrooms need to be cooked a full 10 minutes to destroy any harmful enzymes/bacteria.) Cook over a low heat to retain the golden orange color. Remove from pan and set aside. Add remaining T. of oil to pan, add shallot and garlic, cook one minute, then add rice, stirring to coat. When rice has taken on a pale color, add wine. Stir constantly until wine is fully absorbed. Add ½ cup of hot broth, stirring until absorbed. Repeat until all the broth is used and the rice is cooked al dente.

Remove from heat and stir in the mushrooms (and all that wonderful juice), butter, ½ the cheese. Garnish with remaining cheese and chives.

The risotto itself should take 30 minutes, perhaps a little longer to prepare.

RICE PILAF

It's almost embarrassing how simple some of these dishes are, and this is one of those. Again, we are looking to keep the food interesting and varied.

- 1 cup long grain rice
- 2 cups chicken broth
- 1 can mushrooms, or wild, precooked
- 1 cup frozen peas

Cook the rice in the broth until tender, add the mushrooms and peas, and heat. Serve warm. If there is any left at the end of the meal, this can be added to the soup pot on the stove.

POTATO SMASH

Incredibly simple! Make one for every serving.

- New potatoes
- Butter or olive oil
- Parmesan or Asiago cheese

Preheat the oven to 350°.

Precook the potatoes. I really like Yukon golds for this but any new potato will work just fine. Set the potato on an oiled baking sheet and flatten with a fork or mini masher, but just once or twice to break the skin and squash it. This isn't mashed potatoes. Salt and pepper the pile. Put a pat of butter in the center, and a healthy pinch of cheese.

Bake for 15 minutes, or until cheese browns. This will be crusty. Lift off the baking sheet with a metal spatula.

ASIAN RICE

There are a lot of different things in this dish and they all have their own distinct taste. I serve this as a main dish the first night and a side dish the next day – IF there is any left.

- 3 cup water
- 1 ½ cup long grain rice
- 2 eggs, scrambled, cooked, chopped
- 1 cup fresh, cooked peas
- 1 large onion, chopped
- 1 stalk celery, chopped
- 1 green pepper, chopped
- 1 carrot, peeled and shredded
- 1 cup fresh mushrooms
- ½ cup Bacon, sausage or ham, cooked, chopped (amount can vary depending on what you have)
- 1 T. chicken bouillon
- 2 T. oil
- 2 T. soy sauce

Cook rice in water, set aside. Heat oil in Dutch oven, and stir fry carrots and celery. Add onions and heat through. Add green pepper and mushrooms. Cook until mushrooms start losing liquid. Add rice, bouillon, and soy sauce. Mix well, adding more soy if desired. Add peas, eggs, and meat. Serve warm.

LATE WALK

One evening after dinner, Pete and I took our evening cocktails and ventured forth on our usual late walk. Fortified with good food and drink, and a hard day of work, the walk was slow and casual. We were sticking to the main drive, the original old logging trail, which turned out to be a good thing....

We got about halfway to the main road when we noticed the daylight was starting to fade. In the woods, it gets dark - VERY dark, and very quickly. We turned around and picked up our pace, but it was too late.

Ever since I first saw the property, I could feel the energy all around me, the spirits of the land were happy to see me, happy that I had joined them there. Never once did I feel uncomfortable being alone, for I never felt alone. It's hard to explain, but I felt almost protected by what was around me and I could call on it to reassure me at any time. This is what I did that evening. I pushed my senses out around me and called out with my heart to my woods to guide me home.

I took Pete's hand and said 'just trust me'. I led him at a slow but steady pace through the blackness of the night, right down the middle of the road. I turned us when there was a curve, kept us from stumbling into the side brush, never slowing my pace. When we arrived to the hard left turn that led up to the house, I stopped, and turned Pete to see the light in the window, 50 yards away. He dropped my hand as if it were on fire and said "You're spooky..."

PASTRIES AND SWEETS

I consume little to no refined white sugar. It is my personal belief that it is very bad for the body and eventually causes a multitude of problems and illnesses and that is why this is a short chapter. Eating should be healthy.

PIE DOUGH

Everyone claims to have a foolproof pie dough and I'm no exception. Truly, this one has never failed me. The key to good, tender dough is to *not* handle it! By using a hand mixer, you can work quickly and touch the dough very little. This recipe is easily doubled or tripled.

SINGLE CRUST:

- 1 cup flour
- ½ tsp. salt
- 1/3 cup shortening
- 4 T. water

Combine flour and salt in a bowl. Cut in shortening with an electric mixer on medium speed until dough resembles small peas. Turn the mixer on high and add water all at once. Blend rapidly, about ten seconds. Dough should be a little sticky. Clean the beaters and form a ball with the dough. Remember, handle it very little!

Tear two pieces of waxed paper, 15" long. Lay one on the work surface and put ¼ cup of flour in the center. Place the dough on the flour and slightly flatten with your hand. Turn dough over and cover with remaining paper. Roll dough to desired size. Remove top paper and using *bottom* paper, fold in half. Peel back paper and again, using the bottom paper, fold in half again. Remove paper. The dough is now easy to move to the pie plate. Place point of dough in the center of plate and carefully unfold. Trim edges, flute if desired. Fill and bake.

To use as a baked shell, prick with a fork and bake in 450° oven for 10-12 minutes.

Variations: If making a fruit pie, such as apple or pumpkin, add ½ t. cinnamon to the flour, or any spice that's in the recipe.

PUFF PASTRY

Yes, it's much, much easier to buy puff pastry, but there may come a time when it's not available. This is a light and delicate dough with layers that are created with butter. It can be used to wrap meat, chicken, or fish for a really impressive presentation. It can also be used for making fruit cups.

- 1½ cup flour
- ½ tsp. salt
- ¼ cup plus ½ cup butter (do not use margarine in this recipe)
- 5-6 T. cold water

Stir flour and salt together. Add the ¼ cup butter and cut in with mixer until the size of small peas. Add the water all at once and mix on high. Clean beaters and form a ball. Up until this point, it's much like regular pie pastry. Now it gets interesting! On wax paper, form the dough into a square, smoothing the edges; wrap the wax paper around it and chill for 30 minutes.

Roll out the dough until you have a 12" square. Dot two-thirds of the dough with the remaining ½ cup of butter. Fold the unbuttered edge in first over the center, then the buttered edge, forming three layers. Fold again, top one-third down and bottom up, making a small square. Roll out into a 12" square, and repeat folding sequence. Chill for at least 30 minutes or until you're ready to use. If it's difficult to roll, let it rest and warm a bit.

To use, roll out and cut in desired shapes.

For fruit cups, cut circles with a biscuit cutter and press into a muffin tin or cut small squares and press into a muffin tin with the corners hanging out, bake at 350° for 20 minutes. For salad bowls, cut larger and drape over upside down ramekins on a cookie sheet.

MRS. MANLEY

Back when I first moved to 'the country', I didn't know very much about very much. But I was a willing and apt student for the elderly woman who lived next door. Now, "next door" was a quarter of a mile away, and it was a real effort for her to walk over to my place just to teach me how to make a pie. So, Mrs. Manley, I thank you. I learned well.

The most important thing Mrs. Manley taught me was to not handle the dough too much. The next was to be flexible. I watched in awe as she tossed chopped rhubarb into the raw pie crust and scooped out sugar from my canister. She never once measured anything! After putting the top crust on, she actually poured milk in her hand and spread it over the whole thing, then sprinkled it with more *unmeasured* sugar! It was the best pie I ever had.

She had also tossed in what looked like about two tablespoons of instant tapioca pudding. When I asked about that, she said my boys didn't need more sugar, that boys were active enough as it was. When I pressed, she explained that sugar is a thickener in pies as well as a sweetener, and the tapioca takes up the thickener role. I've used it in almost every 'juicy' pie I've made since, not being overly fond of sugary tastes.

FREEFORM PIE DOUGH

Definitely not a traditional pastry crust! This is made with yeast. For the filling apple and most tree fruits work well and, well, pumpkin doesn't work at all.

- ½ cup warm water, plus 3 T.
- 3 T. instant potato flakes
- 1 T. sugar
- 2 tsp. dry yeast
- Dash of salt
- 1 ½ cup flour

Mix water and yeast and let stand 5 minutes. Add potato flakes, salt, and ½ cup flour. Blend well. Add flour half cup at a time until too stiff to stir. Knead in the bowl a few times, adding small amounts of flour as needed. Total kneading time about 5 minutes. Add a dash of oil to the bowl and turn to coat the dough, cover, and let rise 1 hour. Roll dough out into a 16" circle, then carefully transfer to a greased baking sheet. Pile with your favorite filling and pull edges up, pinching together to make a 10" pie form, leaving the center open to let the steam escape. Bake at 350° for approximately 30 minutes.

APPLE PIE FILLING:

- 6-8 Granny Smith apples, peeled, cored, chunked
- ¾ cup sugar
- 1 T. instant tapioca
- 1 t. cinnamon
- ½ tsp. salt
- ½ cup chopped walnuts (optional)

Mix everything together and pour into pie crust/form. If using basic pie dough, use double crust, one for the top.

STRUDEL

Many years ago, a neighbor gave me this recipe, translated directly from her mother's Latvian cookbook. It was so fun to read that I've left in some of the more interesting directions.

"You need three things to make a good strudel: a large table, a clean tablecloth and lots of patience."

On a board put 2½ cups sifted flour. Make a well in the center. Put a slightly beaten egg in the well. Add some salt and 3 T. olive oil. With a fork, start mixing, working from the center out. Gradually add 2/3 cup warm water and mix only until flour is moistened and water is all absorbed. Dough will be wet and sticky.

"Now the fun starts – pick up the dough and give it one hundred thrashings." (Throw the dough on the board in rapid succession.) At first the dough will be sticky, after beating it won't. If dough is still sticky after the one hundred thrashings, keep going. Do not use any extra flour on your board or hands. Work fast, the dough must not rest during this process. Leave the dough on the board, slightly oiled, and covered with a warm bowl for 30 minutes.

Place tablecloth on table and sprinkle with flour. Place dough in center. Start stretching and pulling, very gently so as not to tear, until dough covers table (it will be very thin). Let rest 10 minutes. Paint dough with melted butter. Spread desired filling over 2/3 area, 3" from edges. Lift edge of tablecloth near the filling and let strudel roll toward you. Pinch ends so filling doesn't come out. Place on pan, forming a circle or an 's'. Brush with butter and bake at 375° for 40 minutes, brushing with butter several times.

WHEW!

APPLE FILLING

¼ cup butter, melted. Add 1 cup dry bread crumbs, 2 cups peeled chopped apples, ½ cup sugar. Cook until apples are tender. Add ½ cup chopped walnuts and ½ tsp. cinnamon. Cool before using.

COTTAGE CHEESE PIE

This has an almost custard-like texture that will quickly become a favorite. It's wonderful plain, but add fresh fruit on top for a delightful change.

- Single pastry crust, page 110
- 3 eggs beaten
- 1 cup sugar
- 12 oz. carton of small curd cottage cheese
- 2 tsp. vanilla
- ½ tsp. salt
- 1 cup evaporated milk
- Walnuts (optional)
- Cinnamon

Mix eggs, sugar, vanilla, and salt. Stir in cottage cheese. Stir in milk. Make a layer of walnuts (chopped or whole) in the bottom of the unbaked pastry shell, and carefully pour mixture into pan. Sprinkle with cinnamon and bake at 375° for 1 hour or until a knife comes out clean.

I have found it easier to move the full pie dish to the oven if I put it on a cookie sheet first, plus it catches the drips.

Toppings, if desired: Sliced strawberries, lightly crushed blueberries, mixed raspberries and blackberries.

BISCOTTI

These quickly became my favorite for coffee dunking. This is a hard, dry cookie with a very distinctive curved shape. The scent of these baking is worth the effort. My favorite is the almond, with its heavenly aroma, but you can use whatever flavoring you like best.

- 2 ½ cups flour
- 1 cup sugar
- ½ cup slivered almonds, chopped
- ¾ tsp. baking soda
- ¼ tsp. salt
- ½ tsp. vanilla extract
- 1 tsp. almond extract
- 3 eggs

Preheat oven to 350°.

Combine dry ingredients in a bowl. Mix vanilla, almond, and eggs together, and then add to dry ingredients, stirring until well blended. Mixture will be dry. Turn the dough out onto a lightly floured surface and start kneading. You will need to get your hands in there and squish it together. Keep going, it *will* stick together, but it's work. Shape dough into a 16" log on a greased baking sheet. Press down gently until 1" thick, shaping sides with your fingers to make smooth. Bake at 350° for 30 minutes. Cool on a wire rack for 10 minutes. Cut roll cross-wise into ½" slices and place cut side down on the baking sheet. Bake another ten minutes. Turn cookie over and bake an additional 10 minutes. Let cool completely on a wire rack. Cookies will be slightly soft in the center, but will harden as they cool.

FRUIT FOCACCIA

- Basic bread recipe, page 83
- ¼ cup sugar
- Jam or fresh fruit
- Milk
- 1 T. sugar
- 1 tsp. cinnamon

Prepare basic bread dough recipe with an increase in sugar to ½ cup for sweeter dough. After the rising, divide in half. Press the dough onto a pizza pan. Spread the jam thickly over the dough, being careful not to get any on the edges. If using fresh fruit, like apples or peaches, dice in one inch pieces. If using seedless grapes (my favorite) do not cut.

Wet the edges with water. Roll out the remaining dough and gently place it on top, lightly pressing the dough down around the fruit and sealing the edges. Pierce the top a few times to allow the steam to escape. Brush the top with some milk and sprinkle with sugar mixed with cinnamon to make the top sparkle.

Preheat the oven to 375° while the focaccia is rising.

Bake at 375° for 30 minutes or until bottom is golden.

Allow to cool slightly, but warm is the best way to eat this.

SWEET ROLLS

Sweet rolls are a wonderful treat any time of day. Nothing says home and comfort food quite like the heavenly scent of bread and cinnamon baking.

- 1 cup warm (not hot) milk
- ¼ cup warm water
- ½ cup sugar
- 1 T. dry yeast (or one packet)
- 1 tsp. salt
- 1 tsp. cinnamon
- ¼ cup softened butter
- 2 eggs, beaten
- 3-4 cups flour

The very first step is to make the dough. Prove the yeast with the sugar, water, and yeast. Then add everything else. Knead for 5 minutes and set to rise for 1 hour. Punch down and let rise again, 1 hour. During the second rise, assemble the filling.

- 1 cup sugar
- 1 T. cinnamon
- ½ tsp. ground cloves, allspice, plus a pinch of nutmeg (all of these are optional)
- 1 cup chopped walnuts
- 1 cup raisins
- ½ stick of butter, melted

Mix the sugar and spices together in a bowl and set aside.

Preheat the oven to 350°.

Once the dough is ready, put it on a lightly floured surface and roll it out into a rectangle, ½ inch thick. Using a pastry brush, paint the dough sparingly with the melted butter. Avoiding one long edge, sprinkle the surface evenly with the sugar mix, nuts, and raisins. Paint the one edge with water.

Now comes the fun part. Starting with one long edge, roll the dough into a long tube. Cut into 2" pieces and place, cut side up, on a greased cooking sheet, not quite touching. Cover with a towel and let rise for 30 minutes, or until double in size. Rising will push the rolls close together.

Bake at 350° for 30 minutes. Paint the hot rolls with the remaining melted butter.

OPTIONAL GLAZE: *1 cup of powdered sugar, water. Put sugar in a small bowl and add 1 T. of water at a time, stirring constantly until you have a thick mass. Using a spoon, drizzle this over the hot rolls.*

A fun and delightful alternative is to pinch off ping-pong ball sized chunks of dough, dip into the butter, roll in the cinnamon sugar, and place in a bread pan. Rise until it crests the pan and bake at 375° for 40 minutes. To eat, just pull off a chunk. The butter coating keeps the bread from 'growing' back together.

CRACKER BARS

This is one of my favorite ways to use the maple syrup I make every spring. I'm not a fan of really sweet things, but this is so good.

- 2 sticks of butter
- ½ cup evaporated milk
- 1 cup maple syrup
- 1/4 cup brown sugar
- 2 cups graham cracker crumbs, recipe on page 38
- 1 package of saltine cracker or soda crackers, recipe in Snacks
- Chocolate, grated

Melt the butter in a pot; add the milk, syrup, brown sugar, and the graham cracker crumbs. Blend well and cook for 5 minutes.

In a 9 × 13 inch pan create a layer of the soda crackers (or saltines), then pour one half the cooked mixture over them; add another layer of crackers. Reheat the remainder of the sugar mixture so it is very hot and pour it over the final layer of crackers. Quickly sprinkle the chocolate on the hot mixture so it can melt. Chill and cut along the cracker perforations.

ANGEL WINGS

These are a special Polish treat. This recipe, however, comes from a very dear Russian friend. Of course, her idea was that most of the vodka went into the cook, not the bowl!

- 2 whole eggs
- 10 egg yolks
- 1 tsp. vanilla
- 2 tsp. baking powder
- 1 ½ oz. vodka (rum for the Polish style)
- 1 cup sugar
- Dash of salt
- 3 cup flour
- Powdered sugar for dusting
- Oil for deep frying

Using a wooden spoon, mix everything in a bowl *except* the flour. (An electric mixer does not work well with this recipe.) Let stand 5 minutes. Add half the flour and mix it in. Then turn it onto a board dusted with the balance of the flour. Mix with your hands until knead-able, and then knead until not sticky, adding small amounts of flour if necessary to keep it from sticking to the board. Roll out into a rectangle, 12 × 18″, cut into 36 small rectangles 2 × 3″. Cut an opening in the center, lengthwise, 1½″ long and turn dough back and through itself. Place on floured board after turning. Deep fry until golden. Frying is very quick so watch carefully. Dust with powdered sugar.

VARIATION: *I've seen this done with five whole eggs and 4 egg yolks. Still a rich pastry and a little easier on the cholesterol.*

SCONES

This is not a very sweet biscuit, but it sure is tasty and goes well with morning coffee or afternoon tea. If you wish something a bit sweeter, smothering it with homemade jam works!

- 2 cup flour
- ¼ cup packed brown sugar
- 2 tsp. cinnamon
- 1 ½ tsp. baking powder
- 1 ½ tsp. baking soda
- ½ tsp. salt
- 3 T. cold butter
- 2/3 cup pitted dates, chopped
- 2/3 cup sour cream
- 1 egg

Combine flour, sugar, cinnamon, baking powder, baking soda, and salt in a bowl. Stir to blend. Cut in butter until mixture looks like small peas. Add dates and toss well. Add sour cream and egg, stirring just until dry ingredients are moistened. Dough will be sticky. Turn dough out on to a lightly floured surface. With floured hands, knead lightly, three or four times. Flour hands again and pinch off dough to make ten balls. Lightly spray a baking sheet and place balls apart, then lightly press down. Bake at 350°, approximately 20 minutes. Serve warm.

VARIATIONS: *Replace chopped dates with: raisins, dried chopped apricots, dried cranberries. Add some chopped nuts. Try using plain yogurt instead of sour cream.*

BISCUITS

Can't have sausage gravy and biscuits without the biscuits! Bread was the first thing I baked in my wood stove, these were the second. Makes 8 biscuits.

- 2 cup flour
- 2 T. baking powder
- 2 T. baking soda
- ½ tsp. salt
- 1 tsp. yeast
- 1 T. sugar
- 2 T. butter
- 2/3 cup milk

Place all the dry ingredients in a bowl. Using an electric mixer, stir on low for five seconds to blend well. Add the butter and mix on medium until the mix looks like coarse meal. Add the milk all at once and blend on high, scraping the sides until all the flour is absorbed, approximately ten to fifteen seconds. This should be done quickly. Scrape the beaters and form the dough into a ball, touching as little as possible but enough to get it into one mass, kneading lightly. Cover and let rest for 15 minutes.

Preheat oven to 450°.

On a floured board, roll or pat dough into a rectangle ½ to ¾ inch thick and five inches wide. Cut down the middle lengthwise, and then in half and in half again in the opposite direction. You should now have eight biscuits and no waste.

Place on an ungreased baking sheet an inch apart and bake for 10-12 minutes or until golden.

OPTIONS: *Use a 2" cookie cutter to make round biscuits. Press the scraps together and cut again.*

POTATO DUMPLINGS

These are the essence of old time cooking and can be cooked in any gravy. Chicken and dumplings is my favorite.

- 5 potatoes
- 1 cup flour
- 1 egg, beaten
- 1 tsp. salt

Peel and grate the potatoes using either a hand grater or a food processor and place in a bowl. Add the egg and salt and stir well. Add the flour and mix. This will be thick and gooey. Bring your soup or stew into which you will be placing the dumplings to a boil, and using a ¼ cup measure, drop balls of dough into the soup. Cook 10 minutes uncovered, then cover and cook an additional 10 minutes.

COOKING OPTIONS: *Drop dumplings into boiling water and cook. These can then be served separately.*

OPTIONS: *Add some shredded or grated cheese before adding the flour. Add your favorite herb.*

FEATHERS AND FUR

As I look back at my time in the woods, one of the things that I miss most and that brings me the fondest memories are the animals. The list of when and where I saw what animal has long been gone, but not the images. From the first deer, to the raccoons, beavers, foxes, pine martens and fishers, the bears, moose, and even a big cat (heard it, found its paw prints, but never saw it), they all have a deep part in my memory, and a special place in my heart.

The birds were ever changing. At last count there were over forty different species, from chickadees to a huge snowy owl, from woodpeckers to a sharp shinned hawk. I enjoyed watching them all. One winter, having the chickadees accustomed to a certain feeding spot, I waited until they had fluttered around at an empty feeder for a short time. Even though the temperature was below freezing, I removed my glove and offered the desired sunflower seeds on my bare hand. I stood stock still for perhaps 10 minutes, and when I was close to giving up, a bird landed on my hand! It took a seed and flew off. Then another landed and another and another, all taking a seed and leaving the sensation on my hand of their weightlessness. Oh, my.

One of my favorite songbirds is the hermit thrush, and I would walk in the mornings and the evenings just to listen to their crystal like songs. It's one you will never forget if you ever are lucky enough to hear it.

The first summer camping on the property, I heard my first cat. We were sitting around the campfire and we heard a screech. A cat - a BIG cat! Pete disagreed, but I'm a cat person and I knew a cat when I heard one. The next morning, a hundred yards or so up the road, were paw prints - clawless paw prints. I could fit my hand inside the print. A very big kitty! Never saw it, but heard it many times throughout the years.

One snowy fall, two young deer wandered up the front yard and found the remains of my small salad garden that I kept near the herb beds. The lack of fear being next to a dwelling was astounding.

One fall the bears were out with their young. It's often been said to not get between a mother bear and her cubs, but what do you do when those cubs are playing on your front porch? Watch! One of the cubs was exceedingly curious and was trying to peek into the house at the glass door. I'm sure the idea of glass escaped it. As I watched from safely inside, it would get closer and closer, and then bump its nose on the glass and back up, confused. Then it would get close again, only to bump its nose once more. It did this a number of times, until it heard me laughing from inside. Bears have very sensitive noses, very poor eyesight, and very good hearing!

The last spring I spent in the woods gave me my most memorable bear encounter. My old cat Muffin loved to sit in the herb bed, basking in the sun. Being mostly deaf and partially blind, she didn't go out alone and I would sit with her. One afternoon as I sat on the top step of the porch reading, I caught a movement in my peripheral vision. Coming out of the woods into the clearing that was the front yard, was a bear. A BIG bear. Easily five hundred pounds, he had a shiny black coat, very healthy looking. Once again I found myself mesmerized by the nature around me. I froze. Muffin was totally oblivious to the drama unfolding. The bear lumbered to the fire pit, but nothing interested him there. Eventually, he came to the herb and flower garden and the first landing of the stairs, not twenty feet from me. I still sat perfectly still. During my seven years in the woods, I learned that most of nature's creatures were not aggressive and would do me no harm. The bear sniffed at the flowers and wandered off toward the driveway, crossing Muffin's vision. She froze, ears and body suddenly at attention! As the bear rounded the corner, now out of sight, I reached down and scooped her up. Five quick steps put her in the house and I grabbed the camera. I leaned around the corner of the high deck until I could see the bear, whose attention now was on the bird seed. *Click*. The shutter of the camera hit the sensitive hearing of the bear and he was gone like a shot. But what a memory.

Then there were the fox cubs that came up the ravine behind the house, so cute! And the pine marten that tried to drag off chicken bones I had left for it, only they had frozen together and it was too heavy to carry. The marten dragged it backward across the snow, stopping to rest occasionally, until I couldn't see it anymore. And the coyotes that would sing to each other all summer long. And, and, and..... *sigh*...

When the snow was all but gone from the woods, the deer would return along their usual paths, one which trailed across just off the front yard. Early in the morning I would go out and put a scoop of sunflower seeds on the bird feeder for our feathery friends, and then I would get a scoop of dried corn. As I walked slowly toward the salt block I had set out, I would shake the scoop, the signal to "my" deer. She was always around at that time and we were friends. She would follow me off to one side, and as I sprinkled corn around the area, she would scurry up to get her share. Not too far behind her were a slightly younger doe and an even younger one: a generational family. With her in the lead, the others came to share the bounty. This doe came year after year. How do I know? All I had to do is shake the corn in the scoop and she would come running to me. A wild animal. Awesome.

The third year of our mutual meetings, I decided I would test how close I could actually get to Sara (of course I had named her by then). One morning after spreading out her breakfast, I backed away and sat down on a log, about twenty feet away. She completely ignored me, but the youngster stomped its feet at me in an act of bravado. I think it was a young buck... they do that. The next morning, I did the same, just to get them used to me not leaving. After a week, I backed up only ten feet, and just stood there. I watched, mesmerized as they all ignored me. Again, I repeated that distance until one morning when I stood there, two more deer showed up, then three more, and they started challenging each other for the food. With hoofs hitting and nips at the young ones, I was way too close to the action and backed away. Experiment over.

Part of our agreed routine was in the late afternoon. Sara would come around alone and stand at the salt block, staring at the house until I noticed her and went out with another scoop of corn. This gave me another idea. I put a little corn on the ground and stood only five feet away, scoop held out. When she finished the small offering on the ground, Sara sniffed the air, and cautiously ventured forward and ate out of the scoop. The feeling of hand feeding a wild animal is one that is very unique and hard to describe.

When the house was for sale, and I hadn't lived there for several months, I had to meet the realtor there. We stood talking on the front porch, and I glanced up. There was Sara, staring at me from her spot at the almost gone salt block. I had trained her to trust me, and I had deserted her. Through the tears, I quickly checked in the basement to see if there was any corn, only to disappoint both of us. It broke my heart. I never went back to the house after that, it was too painful for me to see all I was losing.

After closing on the house, I met with the new owner and told him about Sara. He continued to feed her as I had done. Several years later I asked him about her. It seems that he fed her for about five years, and then one year she was gone and never came back. I'm going to believe that after all the many years I and then the new owner had taken care of her, Sara just got old.

VENISON, FISH AND CHICKEN

VENISON AND BEEF

VENISON NECK ROAST

This is going to be difficult to describe. I learned many years ago how to fillet a fish from its bones, yet leave the fish intact for stuffing. I used the same principle for removing meat from difficult bones like a neck. Most of the time, cooking a venison neck would mean baking the neck, bones and all, and then removing the bones from the tender meat before serving. That doesn't work if you want to stuff it.

Starting at one spot, slice the meat from top to bottom, and then using a very sharp, pointed knife start cutting the meat away from the bone. This is a slow process and the meat will be full of spaces/holes. (Save the bones for soup). Once you have this done, lay the meat on a board. Measure three lengths of cook's string the size of the meat plus twelve inches. Slide these strings under the meat. Push the meat together where it separates.

THE STUFFING:

- 2 slices bread, broken into small pieces
- Salt and fresh ground pepper to taste
- 1 T. dried basil
- 1 small onion, diced
- 1 stalk celery, diced
- ½ stick butter

Ramp greens or other firm green such as collards

In a bowl, toss together the bread, salt and pepper, and basil, set aside. Melt butter and sauté onion and celery 5 minutes or until softened, and add to the bread. Mix well. Using the greens, place an overlapping layer on the meat, add the stuffing on top, and then roll the meat and tie with the strings. The greens keep the stuffing from 'leaking out'. *Note: the ramp greens add a wonderful flavor, however, if they aren't available, any other type of green will work.*

Place the meat in a roasting pan. Add one half cup of water and one half cup red wine. Cover and slow roast at 325° for 3-4 hours. Slice before removing strings. Use the juices to make gravy. As an option, I like adding a can of mushrooms to the gravy for some extra body.

PASTIES

These delightful and tasty hand-held meat pies have a long and rich history in the Upper Peninsula that coincides with all the mining that is done here. It's said that the miner's would take their lunch down in the mine with them, wrapped in a cloth towel. They would then use the towel to hold onto the rich hand-held pie to keep their dirty hands from it. Sounds reasonable to me. Pasties are done with either yeast dough or pie dough. I prefer the flakey pie dough. Rutabaga is a traditional ingredient, although it can be left out. An interesting note here is that the filling is all root crops, with the exception of the meat. Why? Because they were the easiest to store fresh in a root cellar and were used in cooking all winter and into the spring.

THE DOUGH:

- 4 cups flour
- 1 tsp. salt
- 2 cups solid shortening (like Crisco)
- 12 T. (6 oz.) water

Put the flour in a deep bowl and stir in the salt. Add the shortening and with a hand mixer on medium speed, blend until it resembles small peas. Add the water all at once and blend with the mixer on high, just until everything is combined. Do not over mix. I prefer to measure the dough in three ounce balls all at once. Set aside on a lightly floured towel.

THE FILLING:

- 1 pound chopped cooked meat (this can be hamburger, venison, even chicken)
- 1 carrot, diced small
- 1 potato, diced small
- 1 onion, diced small
- 1 rutabaga, diced small

  Mix these together and set aside. Preheat the oven to 375°.

To assemble, roll out one ball of dough 1/8 inch thick (on a floured surface) in a circle; Using a pastry brush or your finger, apply water to the outer edge of the circle. Place maybe ¼ cup of filling on one half and fold the other half over, sealing the edges together. Place on an ungreased baking sheet and continue until done. Bake at 375° until golden brown, approximately 30 minutes. These can be eaten plain, with catsup or with gravy.

SPICED BEEF

This has a lot of steps to it if you're making it from scratch, which is the way I prefer to do it. At the end I will give the alternative method using home canned meat. If I want to impress someone, this is what I make.

- 2 pounds lean beef (or venison), cut into one inch cubes
- 1 large onion, chopped
- 3 garlic cloves, minced
- Fresh rosemary leaves stripped and finely chopped
- 1 bay leaf
- ½ cup flour
- Salt and pepper to taste
- ½ pound mushrooms (wild if you have them) thinly sliced
- ¼ cup cooking oil (add more if needed)
- 1 T. cinnamon
- 1 cup white wine
- Fresh herbs: parsley, chives, rosemary, basil, thyme, oregano (tied together with cooking string to make a bundle.

Put the flour, salt, and pepper in a plastic bag. Add a handful of meat and shake to coat. Heat the oil in a deep, oven proof pot. Brown meat on all sides and remove from pot. Do this in batches so the meat isn't crowded. Repeat until all meat is browned. Add the onions to the oil and cook until wilted, stirring. Add the meat back in plus the mushrooms, garlic, rosemary, cinnamon, herb bundle, bay leaf and wine. Cover and cook over low heat, approximately 30 minutes.

Add enough water to cover the meat, cover, and cook in a 350° oven for another 2 hours, until tender. Stir occasionally, adding more water if it looks dry. Remove the bay leaf and herb bundle. The flour from the meat should thicken for the gravy; if it doesn't thicken to your taste, take some of the flour left over from dredging, make into a paste with water, and add it slowly to the hot juices, stirring constantly.

Spiced Beef from storage is very similar, but the lengthy cooking time is eliminated.

- 1 quart jar of canned lean beef (or venison), cut into bite sized pieces
- 1 large onion, chopped
- 3 garlic cloves, minced or 1 T. from a jar
- Fresh rosemary leaves stripped and chopped
- 1 bay leaf
- 2 cans of mushrooms (or wild if you have them)
- ¼ cup cooking oil
- ½ T. cinnamon
- 1 cup white wine
- Fresh herbs: parsley, chives, rosemary, basil, thyme, oregano (tied together with cooking string to make a bundle. I do this during the summer and either freeze or dry in the bundles)
- ¼ cup flour, salt and pepper to taste plus ½ cup water. Blend smooth.

Add the onions to the oil in an oven proof pot and cook until wilted, stirring. Add the meat in plus the mushrooms including juice, garlic, rosemary, cinnamon, herb bundle, bay leaf and wine. Cover and cook over low heat, approximately 30 minutes. Turn off the heat and let the flavors mingle for 1 hour, or overnight. Remove the bay leaf and herb bundle. Add up to one cup of water if needed. Reheat and add the flour mixture to thicken for the gravy. (If leaving overnight, remove the herb bundle and bay leaf or the flavors will be too strong.)

Either method is served over fresh made pasta, rice or potatoes, with fresh bread and a side salad.

DAVID SAYS: *The spiced beef recipe would be great for Cabernet Sauvignon or an old vine Zinfandel. Because I ALWAYS reach for Cab, I look for meals that compliment OTHER reds, and this one could handle the bold, spicy flavors of a big heavy Zin. The cinnamon and mushrooms will make this a savory meal, and a hearty deep red Zin will be a great compliment!*

HAMBURGER GRAVY

This is a dish that gives me warm feelings and memories. My mother was a good cook and often had to stretch a meal. If all seven of us were present for dinner, she would just make more gravy to stretch the meat. We always had this over mashed potatoes, but serving it on rice or pasta is a great change. Remember, we want to keep the food interesting, not boring.

- 1 pound ground meat
- 1 large onion, diced
- 1 clove garlic, minced
- 1 bouillon cube or equivalent in crystals
- 1 can green peas, drained
- 3 T. flour
- 2 cup milk
- Salt and pepper to taste
- 1 tsp. crushed dry basil

Brown the ground meat in a large pot or skillet until well cooked and then add the onion and garlic; cook until onion is soft. Drain in a colander, reserving the liquid. Add the liquid back into the pot, heat and add the bouillon, dissolving it. Add the flour, stirring to make a roux. Add one cup of milk and stir until thick, add second cup. When the gravy is thick, add the basil and the burger mixture, stirring well. Add the peas last and gently mix in. If the gravy is too thick, add some of the pea juice to thin, otherwise save the juice for soup. Heat through and serve over mashed potatoes, pasta, or rice. Carrot jello on a lettuce leaf makes a nice contrast.

SAUSAGE GRAVY

Knowing how to make gravy is something every cook should learn to do multiple ways. A simple gravy is made of a broth and a flour paste. Sausage gravy is more of a creamy sauce made with the drippings from the sausage. Although you can use less sausage than I use here, I like having lots of meat in it. Also, to make it go further if feeding many, double the recipe.

- 1 pound sausage, mild or spicy to your personal taste
- 2 T. flour
- 2 cups milk

Brown the sausage in a pot or pan. Push the sausage to the side and tip the pan so the grease is in a puddle. Add the flour to the grease, and stir over medium heat. When it bubbles, add one cup of the milk and stir while heating and thickening. Add more milk until it is the consistency you prefer, and stir back in the sausage pieces.

Serve over freshly baked biscuits.

BEEF/CHICKEN WELLINGTON

Beef Wellington is a well-known dish. However, not always having fresh beef when I lived in the woods, I tried the same recipe using chicken and was not disappointed.

Pre-heat oven to 350°.

To make four Wellingtons:

- One puff pastry recipe, page 111, cut into four equal sheets
- 4 tenderloin steaks, 2" thick,
  or two boneless chicken breasts cut in half
- Wild mushroom Duxelle, page 142

Roll out the puff pastry so it will completely cover the meat. Spread 1-2 tablespoons of Duxelle on each sheet to within ½" of the edge. Place meat in the center and fold opposite corners up and pinch to seal. Place on a lightly oiled baking sheet and bake at 350° for approximately 30 minutes, until the pastry is golden.

While the Wellington is baking, sauté additional mushrooms in butter with a splash of red wine. To serve, place equal amounts of sautéed mushrooms on individual warm platters. Lift Wellington from baking sheet with a metal spatula and place on top of half the mushrooms, so the mushrooms fan out from under. Asparagus and carrot coins add wonderful color to the plate.

MUSHROOMS IN THE WIND

One summer I was fortunate enough to meet a professor that taught about mushrooms, and I took one of his classes. My world was forever changed after that weekend. I learned how to identify the different mushrooms that were growing in our area, what was edible and what was not. I got very good at this, and still hunt the wild mushroom to this day.

Certain colors and odors would catch my attention, pull me to them, and I would see these tasty delicacies where no one else would. I spotted the brilliant orange of the Chicken of the Woods that clung to the side of a tree as we were driving one day. We stopped to check it, and seeing that it was in prime condition, I went back to the car for my knife and one of the baggies I now kept handy. Turning back, I was witness to a sight that took my breath away. One of the polypores higher up on the tree was releasing spore… a cloud of orange, a transparent wisp floating from it on a non-existent breeze. A moment difficult to describe, but captured forever in my mind, because once again, I forgot my camera!

WILD MUSHROOM DUXELLE

Many years ago I took a class on wild mushrooming. The class was three days long and worth every minute. It covered how to identify mushrooms, how to take spore samples, where to find what and when. Most importantly, we were taught what *not* to pick. I highly recommend doing this for anyone serious about wild foraging.

One year my mushroom hunting was superb, and I came home with over ten pounds of Oyster mushrooms. I was determined to preserve my bounty and found a recipe for creating a Duxelle— a mushroom paste. With a few changes because of the wild mushrooms, I came up with this remarkable staple.

- 1 pound oyster, chanterelle or other wild mushroom, or any combination
- 1 small onion, diced
- ¼ cup cooking sherry
- 1 T. parsley, plus salt and pepper to taste

Add the mushrooms, onion, and sherry to a blender and puree. Pour this mixture into a fry pan, creating a thin layer, and cook slowly over a low heat, stirring, to evaporate the liquid. When the mushroom paste is thick, stir in the salt, pepper, and parsley, and cool. This can be made in large batches and frozen in one cup packages.

DAVID SAYS: *This meal can pare well with several wines, but I like Merlot as my choice here. The soft, fruit forward Merlot won't overpower the lighter meal, but the mushrooms and flaky pastry will be oh-so-nice with a soft red wine that isn't too heavy.*

STUFFED CABBAGE

My mom was a really good cook. She could make meals out of nothing, or so it seemed. I can only guess that came from growing up during the Depression. She added this and added that, and was hard pressed when I asked for a detailed recipe on her wonderful stuffed cabbage. Here it is. I miss you, Mom.

- 1 cup long grain rice
- 2 T. barley
- 1 ½ cup water
- 1 onion, finely chopped
- 1 green pepper, finely chopped
- 2 oz. salt pork (or bacon) finely chopped
- 2 lbs. ground meat (beef, pork and veal combination)
- 1 egg
- Salt and pepper to taste
- 1 head of cabbage
- 1 quart jar of tomatoes
- Sauerkraut to taste
- Mushrooms optional

Fry together salt pork and onion until soft. Add 1½ cup of water, and bring to a boil. Add the rice and barley. Cook on low for 10 minutes and remove from heat. Rice will continue to absorb water but will not be fully cooked. Cool. Mix meat with egg, green pepper, salt and pepper; gently fold in rice, mixing well.

Bring a large, deep pot of water to boil, and cook cabbage whole, separating leaves as they cook. Cool the leaves and trim the hard vein off. Place ½ cup meat mixture on a leaf and roll up, tucking the ends in. Chop remaining cabbage. Layer rolls on a bed of chopped cabbage and mushrooms in a large roasting pan. Add sauerkraut (Mom always rinsed it); top with the tomatoes. Cover and bake slowly at 325° for 2 hours. Serve with boiled potatoes if desired.

Option: Large collard leaves can be used in place of the cabbage for rolling. Blanch in boiling water 10 seconds and cool.

SPICED KABOBS

Easy to fix, easy to cook, and easy to eat! Grilled skewers of seasoned meat wrapped up in tasty flatbread. Grill over a very hot open fire for crisp meat.

SEASONING:

- ½ tsp. cumin
- ½ tsp. paprika
- ½ tsp. fresh ground pepper
- 1 T. garlic salt
- Blend together and set aside.

KABOBS:

- 1 lb. boneless beef, cut into ¾" cubes
- 2 T. olive oil
- 12 wooden skewers
- Flat bread, page 100

Soak the wooden skewers in water for several hours or overnight. In a zipper type plastic bag, toss the meat with the oil. Add the seasoning and toss well, making sure the meat is well coated. Allow to marinate several hours or overnight. Divide into twelve portions and thread onto skewers, leaving a space between the meat so it can cook more evenly. Grill on a hot fire, approximately 4 minutes on each side or to desired doneness.

Serve hot on flat bread, with thinly sliced red onions and yogurt sauce.

YOGURT SAUCE:

- 1 cucumber, peeled, seeded, finely diced
- 1 cup plain yogurt
- 1 tsp. chopped garlic
- 1 tsp. crushed spearmint
- 1 T. lemon juice

Blend together and chill. Can be made the day before. Stir before serving.

ADVENTURES WITH MICE

If you live in the woods, you're gonna have mice. Fortunately, having two cats kept that problem mostly contained, but there *were* a few incidents....

We had to set mouse traps that first summer. Mice were apparently accustomed to having the house to themselves and weren't quite ready to give up their luxurious accommodations. The cats weren't used to having such lively playthings, and quite frankly, I don't think they understood their job in this matter. So mouse traps it was. I would make sure the traps were set under the wicker plant stand, where the cats couldn't get to the cheese and get their noses whapped. During the night we regularly heard a trap go off, but you can imagine our surprise one morning to see two mice caught in the same trap! It didn't take long for the cats to come around to cooperating and soon the indoor mouse problem was solved.

But not the outside one.

Pete and I loved to fish and looked forward to getting out on the inland lake in the nearest small town. The boat, like all of our equipment, was stored in our large barn over the winter, protected from the elements of the weather, but not from the numerous tiny rodents. Like most men I've known, Pete didn't take suggestions very well, especially when it came to "his" domains. So while we were launching the boat for the first time that season, and I thought it was a good idea to start the motor up *before* we left the dock, I was told in no uncertain terms, "It's fine." We were drifting about 50 yards from shore, and he was having trouble getting the motor started. Eventually it did, and we sputtered even further from shore. Then the engine died. When he took the cover off the motor to check it, a mouse jumped out and into the water, paddling for shore! The mouse startled Pete so that he lurched backward, wrenching his bad back, and dropping the engine cover into the water. I quickly grabbed the fishing net and rescued the cover. While Pete pulled bits and pieces of mouse nest out, dropping them into the water, he could feel his back seizing up. Getting the engine going again was much easier, and we headed back for shore, fishing forgotten.

The mice didn't limit their explorations of our equipment to the boat engine. The first several years, we would park the truck in the barn for the winter, and leave the Jeep at the end of the road. The road from the house to the main road was 1.2 miles and we didn't plow it. Come spring meltdown, we were always anxious to be able to drive the Jeep up to the house. It was quite the event when we could. There would get to be a day when there were enough open spots to make snowmobiling difficult, and that's when the truck came out of the barn. With the ups and downs and curves of the road, there could be a deep drift right next to open gravel. We would drive the 4WD truck through these drifts, exposing the ground underneath, hastening the melting.

One particular spot was always deep snow, and invariably the truck would get stuck. It was my job to shovel what I could, then push while he drove. On one such occasion, the truck stalled. After much difficulty, it started up, and out the tailpipe shot perhaps a cup of burnt corn! Those little rodents at work again.

FISH

SEAFOOD ARUGULA SALAD

As a prelude to dinner, this can't be beat. It could even serve as dinner by making the portions larger.

- 4 strips of bacon
- ½ pound of scallops (halved if large)
- 1 shallot thinly sliced
- 1 T. balsamic vinegar or white wine
- 1 bunch arugula (approximately 6 cups)
- Optional: one slice of prosciutto, cut into six pieces for garnish

Chop the bacon into bits and cook crisp in a fry pan. Remove the bacon and blot dry; set aside. If using prosciutto, cook the pieces crisp and remove from pan; set aside. Add the shallots to the bacon fat, cook one minute, and then add the cleaned scallops and cook quickly, stirring frequently. Remove and set aside.

Add the vinegar or wine to the warm pan, cover for one minute. Scrape up the bits in the pan and reheat. Rinse the arugula and add to the hot pan. Cover and turn off the heat. Let steam for 2 minutes. Remember, we are wilting the arugula, not cooking it.

To serve, divide the wilted greens between four plates, top with the scallops and garnish with the bacon bits and the curled prosciutto. Serve warm.

DAVID SAYS: *A well-chilled Sauvignon Blanc has that crisp light acid fruit that cuts nicely against bacon. Arugula has that bright effect too.*

LINGUINI WITH CLAM SAUCE

This dish is quick, easy, and impressive.

- ½ pound linguini or other long pasta
- ¼ cup lemon juice
- 1 large onion, chopped medium
- 1 T. olive oil
- 2 tsp. chopped garlic
- 1 tsp. oregano
- ¼ tsp. red pepper flake
- 1 cup dry white wine
- 1 can chopped clams (option: home canned fish)
- 1 T. butter
- 1 T. flour
- ¼ cup fresh parsley
- Parmesan cheese, shredded

Start heating the water for pasta. Add pasta and lemon juice when water boils, but continue with recipe so pasta is done when the sauce is finished. Heat oil in saucepan, sauté onion until soft; add garlic, oregano, red pepper, and wine. Cook for 5 minutes. Add clams, including the juice. Cook another 5 minutes; move to a bowl. Melt the butter and add flour, cook to a light roux. Add clam mixture back in and continue cooking additional 5 minutes, until the sauce is thickened. Remove from heat and stir in parsley and ½ cup of cheese. Drain the pasta, place in large serving bowl. Add clam sauce and toss again.

Serve with additional cheese and Italian bread.

SALMON PATTIES

Nothing secret about making these; they're quick and easy.

- 1 can salmon (or home canned fish), drained and bones removed
- 1 small onion, finely diced
- 1 stalk celery, finely diced
- ½ cup bread crumbs
- 1 egg
- ¼ cup mayonnaise
- Milk or water
- Oil for searing

Mash the fish into small pieces, add the onion and celery and toss. Add the bread crumbs and toss again. Add the egg and mayonnaise and mix well. If the mixture isn't wet enough to hold together when you press it into a ball, add some milk or water. Form four balls and set on a plate. Press down gently, forming a patty. Heat oil in a frypan, sear the patties on both sides and remove from pan.

At this point the patties can be chilled until dinner time and reheated for 20 minutes in a 350° preheated oven. If serving immediately, leave in fry pan, covered.

I can't stress enough the importance of presentation. While the salmon patties are very tasty, adding a slice of tomato on top or a big pinch of shredded cheese will turn this into a culinary delight. If you choose to do this, add at the end while reheating so the tomato warms or the cheese melts.

GRAVLAX

This is a cured fish dish. It isn't smoked, it isn't cooked. The salt and sugar cure the meat. Sliced very thin, it's wonderful on crackers or on bagels with cream cheese. I've made it with Coho Salmon, although I prefer Atlantic or Alaskan Salmon for the denser flesh. It's very simple to make, like many of these recipes, although it takes days to finish.

- 1 ½ pounds salmon fillet, skin removed
- 4 T. coarse salt
- 4 T. fresh ground pepper
- 4 T. sugar
- 1 bunch dill fronds

Blend the salt, pepper, and sugar together, set aside. On a large piece of cheesecloth, set the washed salmon slightly off center. With half of the salt mix, evenly coat the fish. Put half of the dill on top and fold the short end of the cheesecloth over the fish to hold the mixture so you can turn it over without losing any. Repeat on the other side and finish wrapping the cloth around the fish.

If you have a plastic baggie, place the fish inside and squeeze out the air so the bag presses against the cheesecloth. Set the baggie on a plate and put another plate on top to gently compress the fish. If a baggie isn't available it can be omitted, but be sure the dish is deep.

Set in the refrigerator for three days to cure. Twice a day, drain away the liquid that will form (and this is why you need a deep dish or the baggie). When the three days have passed, unwrap the salmon and wipe off the dill and pepper blend. If desired, give it a quick rinse. Slice very thin to serve.

SEAFOOD WELLINGTON

There are times in the dead of winter that I crave a taste of summer. That's when I dust off a jar of fish that I caught in August and make a fish pie. Now, that may not sound real appetizing, but you'll change your tune once you've tried it. The puff pastry is the most complicated part of this whole meal, and even that isn't hard. During the winter when I'm snowed in I have plenty of time to spare.

- 1 recipe of Puff Pastry , page 111
- 1 pint jar fish or one can of salmon
- 2 green onions, chopped
- 1½ T. lemon juice
- ½ cup cooked rice (¼ cup dry, plus 2/3 cup water)
- 1½ T. Worcestershire sauce
- Salt and pepper to taste
- 1 egg plus 1 T. water, scrambled

DILL BUTTER:

- 1 cup butter (2 sticks)
- 2-4 tsp. dill, to taste
- 4 T. lemon juice
- Melt butter, add dill and lemon juice.

Cook the rice until tender, rinse, and set aside. Drain the juice from the fish. If using canned salmon, also remove skin and bones and discard. Break into large chunks. Add the onions, lemon juice, dill, rice, Worcestershire sauce, salt, and pepper. Toss gently.

Preheat oven to 400°.

Roll out the pastry and cut into four squares. Place ¼ of the rice/fish mixture in the center of each square. Using the egg plus water, brush the edges and fold the pastry over to form rectangles and seal the edges to enclose the mix. Brush the pies with remaining egg mixture and bake on a lightly greased baking sheet until brown. Cover loosely with foil and bake for a total of 20 minutes. Transfer a pie to a warm plate, top with dill butter, and serve with green beans, steamed carrot sticks, and a slice of tomato.

Serves four.

Options: Any kind of fish can be used, however, if using something that has been frozen, allow to drain first. Adding shrimp or any other seafood really makes this spectacular.

CHEESE STUFFED SALMON

If you love fish as much as I do you're always looking for new ways to prepare it.

- 1 can salmon, drained, cleaned of bones and skin
- 1 egg
- ½ cup fine bread crumbs
- 1 tsp. dried dill
- 1/2 cup feta cheese, crumbled
- ½ cup mozzarella cheese, shredded
- ½ cup fresh greens (spinach, chard, collards, kale)
- Salt and pepper to taste

Lightly separate the salmon in a medium bowl. Add bread crumbs, dill, and salt and pepper, toss. Stir in egg and mix well. Divide into four portions and chill at least 1 hour. Meanwhile, cook the greens, cool, and chop. Fold together greens and cheese, reserving some mozzarella for topping.

Preheat oven to 375°.

Place one portion of salmon between two sheets of plastic wrap and flatten thin. Remove top sheet and slide your hand under, turning over to place on a baking sheet that has been sprayed with cooking oil and remove second piece of wrap. Repeat with a second piece. Place one half of the cheese mix on each piece. Flatten the remaining two pieces and place on top of cheese and seal edges by pressing down lightly.

Bake for 20 minutes. Sprinkle evenly with remaining cheese and return to oven to another 10 minutes.

Serve hot on a bed of rice pilaf with fresh steamed green beans and marinated tomato slices.

STUFFED TROUT

Many years ago I learned to de-bone a (raw) turkey, following the directions in a magazine. The results were nothing short of phenomenal. I utilized what I learned and de-boned a large fish, leaving it whole and intact, like the turkey. I stuffed it, wrapped it in foil, and grilled it. It was amazing and impressive. Here's how.

- 2 trout (of individual serving size), gutted and washed
- Salt and pepper to taste
- ½ pound of wild mushrooms
- Garlic oil
- 4 green onions, sliced diagonally, greens included
- 1 can water chestnuts, drained and chopped
- ½ cup fine bread crumbs
- 1 whole lemon, sliced

To de-bone a whole fish, place fish belly up. Using a sharp, pointed knife (like a Rapala), slide the tip, sharp edge up, under the exposed ribs at the base of the tail. With a slight angle of the knife toward the bone, carefully slice upward. Repeat along the ribs until meat is freed. Using fingers. gently pull bones out, cutting attachments at dorsal, head, and tail. Rinse fish, feeling for and removing any missed bones. Pat dry then salt and pepper to taste. Do not skin.

Prepare your grill.

Wash mushrooms, slice in large pieces, and sauté in oil 10 minutes. Stir in onions, bread crumbs, and water chestnuts. Stuff the fish and secure with toothpicks. Place two slices of lemon on each fish (good time to use the end pieces), and then wrap in foil. Bake about 20 minutes or until tender. Using a wide spatula, lift off the foil and place on plate. Remove cooked lemons and replace with fresh slices.

Serve with rice pilaf and fresh green beans.

DAVID SAYS: *The toughest pairing in the book, because fish usually calls for white wine, but there's a LOT going on here with the stuffing! After some thinking about the ingredients, I decided to stay with white, but I think it would pair up well with a big French burgundy that offers the minerality and flinty clean taste of French burgundy. French Sancerre would also be a nice match.*

ALTERNATE STUFFINGS FOR TROUT

BREAD STUFFING:

- 6 slices dry bread, broken into 1" pieces (depending on the size of fish or how many)
- 1 stalk celery, diced
- 1 small onion, diced
- ¼ green pepper, diced
- ½ stick butter
- Salt and pepper to taste
- 1 tsp. basil, crushed
- ½ tsp. sage, rubbed or finely chopped

Melt butter in saucepan, add onion and sauté 3 minutes; add celery and green pepper, cook additional 3 minutes, remove from heat. Place bread in medium bowl, toss with salt, pepper, basil, and sage. Pour mixture over bread and toss well. If not cooking immediately, do not stuff until you are ready to cook or the stuffing has cooled.

SEAFOOD STUFFING:

- 4 slices dry bread, broken into 1" pieces
- 1 stalk celery, diced
- 1 small onion, diced
- ½ stick butter
- Salt and pepper to taste
- 1 tsp. dill
- 4 oz. seafood (shrimp, crab meat, mock-crab, lobster, scallops, etc.)

Melt butter in saucepan, add onion and sauté 3 minutes, add celery, sauté another 3 minutes, remove from heat. Place bread pieces in medium bowl, toss with salt, pepper and dill. Add chopped seafood and then stuffing mixture and toss immediately.

FISH FILETS WITH TOMATOES

This is a really good way to use inexpensive fish or when you've caught a lot of small fish. The sauce and wine temper any fishy taste. When it comes to mushrooms, use more if you have more.

- 2½ pounds fish
- 3 T. lemon juice or one fresh lemon
- 3 T. butter
- 4 oz. fresh mushrooms, thinly sliced
- 1 tsp. salt
- Fresh ground pepper to taste
- 1 cup white wine
- 4 medium tomatoes, peeled, seeded, diced (or one cup home canned tomatoes, drained)
- 1 cup cooked long grain rice

Heat oven to 350°. Gently toss filets with lemon juice and place in a sprayed baking dish in cross-wise pattern. Melt 3 T. butter in a saucepan and add mushrooms, salt and pepper, then wine. Bring to a boil and pour over fish. Bake for 15 minutes. Pour off liquid into a saucepan. Turn off oven. Cover the fish and put back in oven to keep warm. Cook the fish stock until reduced to 1½ cups. Set aside.

THE SAUCE:

- ¼ cup butter (1/2 stick)
- ¼ cup flour
- ½ tsp. salt
- Dash of cayenne or red pepper flakes
- ¾ cup fresh grated Parmesan cheese

Melt butter in saucepan, add flour, salt and pepper. Remove from heat. Stir in reserved fish stock and then the tomatoes. Cook over medium heat, stirring constantly until thickened. Stir in a half cup of cheese. Pour off any liquid from fish and mushrooms and add liquid to sauce. Stir.

To serve, place warmed fish on fresh cooked rice, top with sauce and remaining cheese. Add fresh green beans.

FOWL PLAY

When my boys were still very young and we lived on a small farm, I learned how to butcher a chicken from a neighbor who lived further down the road. She had a much larger piece of land, a huge garden, goats, a cow, and a big flock of chickens

The opportunity came one afternoon when my husband and I, along with another couple, watched a pheasant run back and forth across the road from inside the house. As soon as someone commented that the dumb bird would get hit if he didn't stop, he got hit. I ran out, grabbed the bird, and headed down to Jean's for my lesson.

She showed me how to feather it in boiling water and then singe the pin-feathers off. She cut off the head and pulled the gizzard out, showing me how to clean it. What an education I had that day. Because the bird had been hit, Jean also showed me how to determine if the meat had been spoiled by the impact by examining the liver and the bile sack. The bird was good. This was after I stuck my hand into the bird and following her directions, pulled out all the innards.

We washed it out and I took my prize home. The four of us adults had a taste of pheasant for dinner that night along with lots of fresh vegetables from the garden.

The same principles apply to butchering a chicken, a considerably larger bird than that pheasant, and I became quite adept at killing, feathering, and gutting birds.

Because I had small children, I made sure that draining the blood from a bird was done in one spot only. I would tie twine to one chicken foot, chop the head off, and then hang it from a crosswise post by tying the other foot and that kept the bird and the mess contained.

Many sayings have a basis in truth and practicality and "Running around like a chicken with its head cut off" always fascinated me, so I tried it – once. The boys thought it funny, but I had a hard time catching that bird until it finally dropped on its own.

CHICKEN

CHICKEN MARSALA FROM STORAGE

I don't dine out very often because I love to cook, but when I do, I usually try something new. Once I had a taste of this, I was determined to figure out how to make it.

I'm going to present it both from storage and fresh. Either way, it's a great variation for meals, and should be served with bread to mop up the yummy sauce.

- 1 pint jar of chicken, chopped, broth included
- 1 can of mushrooms, juice included (or wild mushrooms of your choice, cooked)

THE SAUCE: (see White Sauce, page 186)

- 2 T. butter
- 2 T. flour
- 1 cup milk
- ½ cup Marsala wine
- Sour cream, optional

Melt the butter in a pot deep enough to hold everything, add the flour to make a roux, adding salt and pepper to taste, stirring constantly. Stir in one half of the milk and heat. As it starts to thicken, add the other half. Keep stirring until thick. Add the chicken and the mushrooms; heat while stirring. Once thickened again, add the Marsala. Blend in the sour cream.

Serve over homemade pasta (page 74) cut into narrow ribbons, and fresh bread. A salad is a good addition.

If broccoli is available, a lightly steamed stalk adds wonderful color to the plate.

CHICKEN MARSALA, FRESH CHICKEN

- 1-2 chicken breasts, thinly sliced
- ½ pound fresh mushrooms
- ½ cup flour, seasoned with salt and pepper
- 4 T. butter

Melt 2 T. butter and sauté mushrooms. Transfer to a dish, juice and all. Melt remaining butter in pan. Dredge the chicken in flour and sear in the butter. Transfer to the mushroom dish.

Proceed with the sauce as above.

CHICKEN STUFFED MANICOTTI

This is one of those amazing dishes that is very simple to make and keeps meals from getting boring. This might be a good time to add a word about stress. During a disaster, or any event that adds additional stress to your life, doing something that is normal, like cooking, or even something that is fun, like having friends over to play cards, can be a tremendous stress reliever. This is why I cooked a lot during all the problems we faced.

- One batch of homemade pasta (page 74), cut into 5″ × 6″ sheets
- One pint jar of chicken, drained and diced (reserve juice for soup)
- One small onion, finely diced
- One rib of celery, finely diced (optional)
- Two slices of bread, broken into small pieces
- 1 tsp. basil
- One egg
- Salt and pepper to taste

Combine everything except the pasta and blend. Set aside. Bring a pot of water to boil and add the pasta sheets, stirring gently so they don't stick together. Cook for 2 minutes. Drain and rinse in cold water.

Preheat the oven to 350°.

Taking one pasta sheet at a time lay it on your working surface. Put ¼ cup of meat mixture in an even line, lengthwise on the pasta. Fold over one edge and roll to make a tube. The two edges of the pasta must overlap. If the pasta isn't still wet, put a line of water on the furthest edge so the tube seals. Place the manicotti in a baking dish, seam side down. Repeat until the mixture is used.

Now you cover it with a sauce.

With chicken I like using a garlicky white sauce with Parmesan cheese.

A plain tomato sauce is sufficient, sprinkled with mozzarella or Parmesan cheese, and baked at 350° for 30 minutes to 1 hour, depending on your stove.

Since I have used a wood cookstove for my needs and the temperature fluctuates a great deal, it's difficult for me to be precise on timing. Use your judgement and watch your oven.

CHICKEN PARMESAN

I've had this recipe for so long I don't even remember where I got it from, and it's one of my favorites. I've used it and shared it and modified it. This doubles well, but don't reduce it. Make the full recipe and freeze or can what you don't use.

THE SAUCE:

- 1 medium onion, minced
- 4 cloves garlic, minced
- 3 T. olive oil
- 6 oz. can of tomato paste
- 1 quart jar whole or diced tomatoes
- ½ tsp. *each* rosemary, basil, marjoram, thyme, freshly ground black pepper
- 1 tsp. *each* oregano, salt
- 1 T. maple syrup

Heat 2 T. oil in a large, heavy pot, and sauté onion and garlic for 5 minutes. Add 1 T. oil, heat, and then add the tomato paste and some of the juice from the tomatoes, combining well, and stirring frequently. Add the tomatoes and herbs, and then bring to a boil, stirring constantly. Reduce heat and simmer for *at least* 1 hour, 3-4 hours is even better. Divide sauce at this point if needed.

THE CHICKEN: (FOR TWO)

- 2 boneless chicken breasts
- Milk
- ½ cup *each* fine bread crumbs and grated Parmesan cheese, blended
- 2 T. olive oil
- Mozzarella cheese

Wash chicken, pat dry, dip in milk, and dredge in bread crumb mixture. Heat oil in a fry pan and brown the chicken, turning once. Remove chicken from pan and add to the sauce, spooning the sauce to cover the chicken. Cover and simmer another 15 minutes. Add sliced mozzarella to top of chicken the last 5 minutes or until melted.

THE PASTA:

Cook the pasta of your choice according to package directions. Drain. Add 2 T. balsamic vinegar to chicken fry pan, scraping bits as you heat. Add the pasta to pan and toss with vinegar bits.

To serve, divide pasta onto warm plates, top with chicken and sauce, along with freshly baked Italian bread.

CURRIED CHICKEN

- 1 lb. boneless, skinless chicken, cut into ½" pieces
- 1 large onion, halved and thinly sliced
- 1 clove garlic, chopped
- ½ tsp. powdered ginger
- ½ tsp. *each* red pepper flakes, turmeric, salt
- 1 t. curry powder
- 1 bay leaf, broken
- 1 large tomato, diced (or one pint from storage)
- 2-4 T. cilantro
- 3 T. olive oil

Heat oil in pan and then brown the chicken. Remove from pan and set aside. Sauté onion and garlic. Mix the ginger, cayenne, turmeric, curry, and salt together then add to onions. Add bay leaf. Cook 1-2 minutes. Add the tomatoes and chicken. Cook an additional 15 minutes until thickened and the chicken is cooked. Remove the bay leaf.

Serve over cooked rice, garnishing with the cilantro.

BASIL CHICKEN ON ANGEL HAIR

This is another very easy dish to create for something different. Variety in your meals can go a long way toward keeping boredom from creeping in when you're snowbound or hunkering down.

- One Basic White Sauce , page 186
- ¼ cup fresh basil, chopped
- 1 pound raw chicken, cut into bite sized pieces (or one jar canned)
- 2 T. butter or olive oil
- 1 pound angel hair pasta
- Fresh shredded Parmesan cheese

Sauté the chicken in the butter or olive oil until cooked through. Set aside and keep warm.

Create a thin basic white sauce and then stir in the basil and any juice that comes from the chicken, keep on very low heat, stirring occasionally.

Cook the pasta according to package directions. Drain, rinse with warm water, and drain again. Divide the pasta between the plates, twisting it into a nest. Place a ladle of sauce on pasta, then chicken, then another ladle of sauce. Serve with cheese.

PECAN CHICKEN

I had this dish once at a restaurant and while the taste was fabulous, it was difficult to eat because the honey had caramelized the large pieces of pecans, making it rock hard. I set out to do better.

For each serving:

- 1 chicken breast
- 1 T. maple syrup
- 2 T. pecan meal (or any nut meal) (meal is finely ground)
- 2 T. butter
- Your choice of pasta

Rinse the chicken and pat dry. Set the chicken on a plate and drizzle on half of the syrup, making sure it's fully coated. Turn the breast over and do the other side. Take 1 T. of the meal and sprinkle it liberally over the chicken, pressing the meal into the syrup; turn the breast over and do the other side.

Start a pot of water to cook the pasta.

Melt 1 T. of butter in a frying pan over medium heat and sear the chicken on both sides, turning when the chicken turns golden brown. Reduce heat and finish cooking, approximately 20 minutes. Remove from pan and keep warm. Add the remaining butter to melt, scraping up the bits in the pan.

Cook and drain the pasta and stir into the melted butter. Arrange on a warm plate and top with the chicken. Add some green beans for color and serve.

DAVID SAYS: *Chicken is one of those foods that can go great with red or white, depending on preparation. With the sweetness of maple, and the heavy addition of pecans, I'd go red here. This is served with pasta, so it's an unusual blend of savory flavor and a hint of Italian cooking. I'd probably enjoy an Italian Barolo or even Chianti.... but one great thing about Barolo, if you're going to be storing wine for years, Italian big reds age extremely well.*

MISCELLANEOUS

MY FAVORITE SPAGHETTI SAUCE

Everyone has their own favorite sauce, and I'm no exception.

- 1 lb. ground meat
- 1 medium onion, diced
- 6 cloves garlic, diced coarsely
- 1 sweet green pepper, diced (use red if you can't eat the green)
- 6 oz. can of tomato paste
- 3 quarts jars whole or diced tomatoes
- ½ tsp. *each* rosemary, basil, thyme, freshly ground black pepper
- 1 tsp. *each* oregano, salt
- 2 T. maple syrup
- Options: bone-in chicken breast, bone-in country ribs, medium spicy Italian link sausage

Brown the meat with the onion, garlic, and green pepper; drain fat and discard. Add one quart of tomatoes and the tomato paste, stir until well blended. Add second quart of tomatoes plus all the remaining ingredients. Simmer over low heat 1 hour.

As a delightful addition, add medium spiced Italian link sausage cut into half inch pieces, bone-in country ribs and a bone in chicken breast. Simmer several hours until meat is thoroughly cooked and tender. Remove the ribs and chicken, discard the bones, and dice the meat and return it to the pot. This is best served the next day.

EGGPLANT LASAGNA

My mother fixed fried eggplant on a regular basis. That is the first step in this incredible vegetarian lasagna. You could easily stop there and just eat the eggplant, but these are so good it will be difficult to save some for the recipe.

- 1 large eggplant, peeled and sliced in ½" pieces
- 1 egg, scrambled with 1 T. water
- ½ cup seasoned bread crumbs
- ½ tsp. salt
- 2 T. grated Parmesan or Asiago cheese
- ¼ cup olive oil
- 1 homemade pasta recipe, page 74, cut into 4" × 7" sheets
- 1 spaghetti sauce recipe, page 168, minus the ground meat if vegetarian is preferred
- 1 lb. mozzarella cheese

Mix the bread crumbs, salt, and grated cheese together. Spread the bread crumbs on a plate. Dredge the eggplant in the egg mixture and then into the bread crumbs, coating both sides. Heat oil in a fry pan and cook eggplant until both sides are darkly golden. Remove from pan and set on doubled paper towels to drain. Repeat until all eggplant is cooked.

Pre-heat oven to 350°.

Assembly: Put 2-3 T. of sauce in the bottom of a lasagna pan or a glass bread pan. Add a layer of pasta, more sauce, eggplant (at least two pieces depending on the size you used), more sauce, and then cheese. Repeat until pan is full, ending with sauce and reserving enough cheese to cover. Bake in oven for 30 minutes, remove and add cheese, return to oven and bake additional 30 minutes.

Serve with fresh bread sticks.

STUFFED PORTABELLAS ON ANGEL HAIR PASTA

I prefer using portabellas for this dish because they retain their cup-shape even after cooking. An excellent alternative is the wild Boletus Edulis, Winecap or giant puffball. When it comes to anything wild always know what you're picking! The different fillings are what make the dish and they are endless. Here are a few of my personal favorites. The amount to use will depend on how many caps you are filling. These suggestions fill two caps.

Preheat oven to 350°.

For each person, you will need two caps. If using regular stuffing mushrooms or very small portabellas, double the amount. Sauté in butter, bowl up. As the liquid starts to release, turn mushroom down. Total cooking time is 8-10 minutes. Remove from pan and fill, setting each filled cap on a lightly oiled baking sheet. When complete, set sheet in oven for 5 minutes to reheat and melt cheeses.

WILD MUSHROOMS:

Boletes and Wine caps are prepared the same as portabellas. Giant Puffballs are sliced into 1" thick steaks and then cut into 3" squares and sautéed in butter over low heat, 5 minutes on each side. Pile the fillings on the Puffball.

DICED TOMATOES WITH BASIL AND BALSAMIC:

For taste and presentation I use Black Krim tomatoes or the red and yellow Stripy, but any fresh tomato will do. Dice one tomato and set in a colander to drain for 15 minutes. Fill two caps, drizzle with a splash or two of good balsamic vinegar. Heat. Tear a leaf of fresh basil into pieces and garnish.

FETA WITH SPINACH:

Chop a handful of spinach and sauté with 1 T. butter until wilted. Cool. Split between two caps, add one tablespoon of feta crumbles to each and heat.

CRAB MEAT STUFFING:

This will make more filling than just for two caps. With the remainder, make into patties and freeze for crab cakes.

- 1 6oz. can of crab meat, drained
- ¼ cup seasoned bread crumbs
- 1 tsp. pepper blend #2, page 188
- 1 tsp. Worcestershire sauce
- Dash of liquid smoke
- 1 T. mayonnaise
- 1 tsp. lemon juice
- Parsley for garnish

Mix everything together, stuff into caps. Without the use of egg, this does not require lengthy baking, just heating through. Garnish with parsley.

ONIONS/RAMPS AND MOZZARELLA:

Sauté half of a small sweet onion, toss with ½ cup shredded mozzarella and fill caps. Heat. Whenever possible I use wild ramps. If you have them available, you only need one ramp plus the greens for each cap. Wash and chop the bulb and the greens; toss with ½ cup mozzarella and fill caps. Heat.

ROASTED RED PEPPERS WITH PARMESAN:

Remove one roasted red pepper from a jar, discard any seeds, and dice coarsely. Fill cap and add one tablespoon of fresh shredded Parmesan to each cap. Heat.

THE PASTA:

Cook angel hair pasta according to package directions. While pasta is cooking, in a bowl, add one cup of cream and ½ cup of chopped fresh basil. Stir. When pasta is done, drain and add to bowl. Toss. Divide between the plates and top with mushroom caps. Garnish the plate with slices of radish and strips of orange bell pepper.

DAVID SAYS: *This recipe has so much going on that although I want to reach for another Barolo or Brunello, I HAVE to have a HUGE California Cab. If I had one in the cellar, I'd be pulling the cork on a Silver Oak, Chimney Rock, Faust or some other "huge red" Cabernet Sauvignon. Why? Because this meal is layered in flavors, and so is a huge red. I'm hoping I get invited for dinner when Deborah makes this... this recipe can take a big red every bit as much a steak, roast or lamb chop!*

EGG FOO YUNG

Whenever my mother found a new Chinese restaurant, she would order the Egg Foo Yung. To her, this was the telling dish on whether or not the place was any good. It is basically an egg and vegetable patty, deep fried and served with gravy over rice. It comes in many variations, including shredded pork, beef, chicken, turkey or shrimp or vegetarian.

- ½ lb. meat (your choice, omit for vegetarian)
- 1 tsp. salt
- 1 T. dry sherry
- 1 tsp. soy sauce
- 1 T. cornstarch
- 5 eggs
- 2 T. oil
- 2 green onions, chopped
- 6 water chestnuts, chopped
- 4 oz. fresh mushrooms, sliced
- 1 can bean sprouts, drained and coarsely chopped
- 4 cup oil for deep frying
- Gravy
- Cooked rice

Beat the eggs with salt, cornstarch, sherry, and soy sauce. Set aside. Heat 2 T. oil in a fry pan or wok and sauté onions and water chestnuts for one minute. Add mushrooms and meat (if using) and cook an additional minute. Remove to a bowl and cool. Add bean sprouts and then fold in the egg mixture.

To cook: Heat oil to 400° in a deep pot. Gently ladle a large scoop into the oil, (I use a soup ladle). Deep fry approximately one minute until browned. With a wide wire spatula, carefully turn over and cook the other side. Using the same spatula, remove from oil and move to a platter and keep warm. Repeat. Serve on bed of rice with gravy. Serves four.

Gravy: Heat 2 cups stock (beef or chicken) and 4 T. soy to boiling. Mix 2 T. cornstarch with 2 T. water and add to stock. Reduce heat. Stir until thickened.

HARVEST CASSEROLE

A dear friend shared with me this recipe which was handed down from her great-grandmother, Rebecca. During the fall canning season it was made with anything that didn't make it to the canner.

This is the perfect Prepper's meal. The actual ingredients will vary depending on what you grow in your garden and what you have at the end of the season. There is no waste. If you have only a handful of green beans, cut them into 1" pieces and add.

- 4-6 large potatoes, scrubbed and sliced 1/8" thick
  2 large carrots, scrubbed and sliced
- 2 onions, cleaned and sliced
- 1 cup peas
- 1 lb. ground beef or venison, cooked and fat drained
- Salt and pepper to taste
- 1 quart tomatoes

Using a large, deep casserole dish or a Dutch oven, oil the sides and bottom well. Place a layer of one half of the potatoes, then carrots, onions, meat, peas, remaining potatoes, and then the tomatoes. Cover and bake for 1 hour or until potatoes are soft. Serve in bowls with fresh bread.

Options: Thinly sliced rutabaga or turnips; corn cut from the cob, cut green beans, summer squash.

TIP: *This Can Be made in a disposable deep-dish pan for taking to a potluck or an easy clean up.*

BAKED BEANS

My mom made the best baked beans from scratch. I have her recipe card in front of me. There are few amounts for the ingredients and even fewer for the directions.

- 2 lbs. Great Northern beans
  (rinse and cover with water, soak overnight)
- Salt
- Onion, peeled, left whole
- 3 T. chili sauce
- 1 bottle catsup
- Bacon
- 1 ½ T. brown sugar
- 1 T. molasses

Combine the soaked beans, onion, and bacon and boil until soft, approximately 1 hour. Remove onion and bacon. Do not drain. Add catsup, chili sauce, sugar, and molasses. Spread evenly in a 9 × 12 × 2″ baking pan. Cut bacon into small pieces and lay on top. Bake 2 hours at 275°. Let sit for 30 minutes before serving.

MID-EAST FEAST

It's hard to describe this dining experience. Tradition has one seated on the floor on a pillow at a very low table and you eat with your hands. I prefer to sit on a chair at a dining table, but you still eat with your hands. I've managed to recreate most of the dishes and have added a few of my own. The color contrast here is wonderful. The traditional bread still escapes me, but the crepes are a very good substitute. Because there is so much food here, I would recommend this meal for at least four people, and it's even more fun with six.

There are six separate dishes in this meal, recipes for some of which are found elsewhere in this book.

- A double or triple batch of Crepes, page 98
- Syrian Salad, page 57
- Spiced Beef, page 136
  Lift the beef out of the gravy with a slotted spoon into a bowl, and lightly mash with a fork to shred it.
- Curried Chicken, page 163
  Lift the chicken out of the sauce with a slotted spoon into a bowl, and lightly mash with a fork to shred it.
- **MUNG BEANS**
  - 1 cup dried mung beans
  - ½ onion, diced
  - 1 T. chicken bouillon
  - 2 cups water

  Rinse the mung beans. Add beans, onions, and bouillon with the water in a pot. Bring to a boil and simmer until beans are tender, approximately 2-3 hours, adding additional water if necessary. Lightly mash with any remaining liquid.

- **RED LENTILS WITH RICE**
  - 1 cup lentils
  - 1/3 cup rice
  - 4 cup boiling water
  - 1 tsp. salt
  - ½ tsp. cumin
  - 1/3 cup olive oil
  - 1 onion, halved and thinly sliced

Rinse the lentils in a colander. Add to boiling water, return to a boil, and simmer 1 hour. Add salt and rice, cook another 30 minutes, adding water as necessary. Sauté onion in oil, add to the pot when rice and lentils are tender, then stir in cumin.

- **COLLARD GREENS**
  - 3 cups raw greens, chopped or one pint home canned
  - Salted water
  - 1 tsp. olive oil
  - ½ tsp. cumin

Add greens to boiling water, cook for 5 minutes. Drain and add oil and cumin and toss.

If using home canned greens, pour into a pot to heat. When fully heated, drain and add the cumin.

The crepes, spiced beef, and curried chicken may be made the day before. Reheat the beef and chicken before serving.

To serve the meal, line a round pizza pan with crepes. (The pizza pan allows you to turn the dish for easy access to the other side.) Mound some salad in the center. Fill a one cup measure with one of the dishes and invert onto the crepes, making little piles around the salad. Repeat until all are presented. Serve extra crepes folded in a basket. Set the pan in the center of the table.

To eat, tear a piece of crepe, scoop up some food by pinching the crepe, and enjoy!

SPRING MELTDOWN

It was a long and cold spring that year, very snowy, so when in mid-May the temperatures climbed into the sixties, we basked in the warmth!

On May 18th, with those warmer temps, we decided to go to town together, since the wood fired furnace wasn't running and didn't need tending. There were still several feet of snow in areas, so we packed the sled with laundry, donned the snowshoes, and hiked out to the car.

With light hearts, and faces to the warm sun, we made our way down the road and across the swollen creek that coursed through the five culverts beneath our feet. The snow was wet, soft, and slushy, and made the walking difficult. We looked at it as a wonderful thing: the snow was finally melting in the woods. The air was clean and warm and held such promise.

Pete and I had a great day in town. We did laundry, and folded clothes side by side, watching large puddles and rivulets forming in the parking lot from the melting snow. We did the grocery shopping together, something we rarely did, as that was my job and my expense. I let him pack the purchases his way, knowing every bit of space counted when it was transferred to the sled. We stopped for a casual lunch and had a rare afternoon rum and coke to celebrate our first really warm day.

The sky was a brilliant blue when we parked the car in its snow stall back on our road. I recall commenting how much the banks of snow had gone down during our trek to town, a trek that had lasted only six hours. Earlier on the radio, the excited newscaster had mentioned a rare 85° had been reached that day! This was going to be a wonderful spring. I had high hopes for the coming year with such good omens.

We climbed the snow bank behind the Jeep and slipped into our snowshoes, balancing the sled enough to pull it up where we stood, now less than two feet higher than the ground around the Jeep... the muddy ground, squishy and soggy with melting snow. When we rounded the first curve of the road, it was obvious we weren't going to need the snowshoes. There were several patches of open ground on the road, which meant we would soon be driving in. It was a bit more difficult dragging the sled over the mud instead of snow, but manageable, and we were excited about the quick melt... until we reached the creek.

The water that was under the road was now OVER the road, by quite a bit, and it was flowing fast, really fast. After taking a few pictures (this was the most excitement we'd had in months!!), we discussed a course of action. Pete went back to the Jeep and got some rope. Meanwhile, I scouted around and found two long, sturdy saplings and cut them for walking sticks. When Pete returned, we tied one end of the rope around Pete, looping and tying the rope to the sled, and the end of it around my waist. Pete led the way across the treacherous gully wash, stepping carefully only after probing with the walking stick to make sure there was road under his feet. There were perhaps fifteen feet between him and I with the sled bobbing in the river between us. I stepped into the rush of water. The fast current sucked at my boots and quickly washed over the tops and in, soaking my feet with icy sludge.

It felt like forever crossing that stretch, when in fact it was less than 5 minutes. Safely on the other side, we stopped to empty the water out of the boots, and to ponder what had just happened. We left the cut saplings nearby, in case we needed to cross again. That was not something I wanted to do.

The rest of the walk back to the house was in stunned silence. We put the laundry away, and I dealt with the groceries and started dinner. The only thing we could possibly do was wait until the water receded.

The next morning, with more blue skies and sunshine, we walked back to the creek, never expecting what was waiting for us. The culverts, weighing more than we could even roll, were upended. Some of them had already washed downstream and the river continued to roar past us.

What we did notice that morning was the road from the house was almost completely open, muddy but open, and we could drive the truck to the creek. No further, of course, but it was a start.

At the end of the second day, our curiosity got the best of us, and we took a late ride down to the creek. The river had receded from overflowing the banks, but was still rushing. The culverts were gone. All of them. Of the five, three were within fifty feet of the crossing, one was almost two hundred feet downstream, and the final was in between, crumpled like a flimsy tin can. The power of the water was mindboggling. Apparently, so much debris from further upstream had backed up against the culverts that the force of the water just pushed… until the resistance was gone. There was this gaping hole in our road and no way to get from one side of the road to the other. At least we had one vehicle on either side.

Over the next few days I made several phone calls. The property belonged to the County Road Commission. They still owned a now abandoned gravel pit to our south, and technically that portion of the road was theirs. When I called and asked about washed out roads, I was told it was the responsibility of the landowner, not the road commission, to fix washouts. Then I pointed out that the area in question was owned by the road commission. I was met with silence. He then said he'd get back to me and hung up. I never heard another word from them, of course.

We needed to do something on our own.

The first thing we did was to place several boards from one bank to a large rock, and from there to the other bank and then yet across another to the road: a footbridge. Then it started to rain.

For several days, for hours and hours, Pete and I worked in the rain with his come-along, slowly dragging the culverts back into place. It was quite the process, since the winch only stretched so far. We went through two come-alongs during the process. With the constant, tedious ratcheting, Pete's mind started to wander, and he overtightened the cable, breaking the internal gears. It was time for a new one. With the new tool, we pulled, inches at a time, then move, a few more feet, then move again, until after four days, we had dragged three of the culverts back into place. The furthest was much too far and the damaged one was useless.

Pete started cutting nearby trees and I stripped off the branches. Slowly we built a log bridge across those three culverts. The final addition was 2 × 12 boards, in two strips, to give support to the vehicles. I was terrified the first time I crossed, but I knew that in watching out the side window, as long as I kept that front tire just inside the edge, at a certain spot, the other tires were fine and would follow.

We had access.

Before getting the culverts in place enough to build the simple bridge across them, life in the UP took on the glorious days of an instant summer. The snow was all gone, the sky was a brilliant blue, and the sleepy little town we were near woke and was ready to socialize.

One morning, I got a phone call on the car-bag-phone we had hooked up to the 12 volt battery. Jamie announced there was going to be a bring-a-dish party at Buck's place on Saturday. Bring-a-dish and your own 'liquid refreshment' parties were very typical. There was no burden on anyone for the cost of food or beverages, yet a good time was had by all. Jamie gave me the times, then announced "oh, and Charlie and I are getting married at the party and Buck is officiating". Huh??? Well, that put a new spin on the party.

Having been a cake decorator and putting myself through massage school creating wedding cakes, I decided that would be my gift to the new couple. A few phone calls to the bride's closer friends got me how many would be at the party, what her favorite cake flavor was, and the flowers she would have. I had only three days to pull this off.

First thing on the agenda was to check my supplies for the necessary ingredients for frosting and cake, make a list, and do a quick run to the store. As quick of a run as could be when the nearest store was fifteen miles away, and we were still walking across boards over the creek and dealing with washed out roads.

The day of the wedding arrived, overcast with a light drizzling rain. Pete packed his camera (he was taking the event pictures), and I loaded the cake, in layers, onto a board that went into the back of the truck for the ride to the creek - our transfer point. In the rain, I balanced the cake carefully as I made my way across the slippery foot path, and placed the cake tenderly in the back of the Jeep for the ride to the party. The cake was a big hit and I was 'forgiven' for not bringing a dish to pass when I claimed I brought dessert!

Everyone was amazed at our tales of the washout and how we were managing. We were 'anointed' with honorary local status, since we not only had survived a record breaking winter, but we were staying for the next one. Apparently, many new residents left after the first winter.

Once I got over my initial fear of plunging the Jeep off those two narrow boards and into the depths of the two foot deep creek, I traveled with ease over the makeshift bridge. It was much like getting used to driving through six inch deep puddles for the first time, nothing I had ever done as a city girl, and something I never thought twice about now. I will admit that I felt better about my driving skills when someone else, a local guy, did slip off the boards, and had to get someone to tow his pickup back onto the road.

Later in June, as I was coming back from a shopping trip to town, I was on the long dirt road that led to our private road. I came up behind a very large truck with what looked like bridge pieces on the flatbed. The longer I stayed behind him, the more anxious I became, especially when he turned onto my road. I followed him to the bridge, just in time to see a crew use a logging picker pull up all of our hard work, boards and trees, and dump it off to one side. I parked the car, slamming the door. I instantly knew who was in charge, and went toe-to-toe with him. I asked him what the hell he thought he was doing with MY bridge and hadn't he even stopped to think that someone had built that because *someone lived* here, and why hadn't I been told?? I was livid, and furious at not being informed about what was going on.

Apparently, this logger owned quite a bit of land up behind us, and needed the road and good access to log. When he had first tried to access his property that year, he discovered the washout and our temporary solution. He had gone to the county, obtained the necessary permits to put in a good solid bridge, and was replacing it. This, of course, was to our benefit, but upsetting that we were not informed so we could be prepared for the six hours of no access. I would have just stayed home had I known.

Much to everyone's surprise (and unease), I climbed down the bank of the creek, stepped across stones and up the other side. I could hear the guys snickering over the boss being dressed-down by a 5'5" little gal - a very angry little gal. I jogged up to the house in just a few minutes, told Pete what was going on, and we drove down to the bridge to retrieve the groceries and so he could see I wasn't exaggerating about the events.

While we loaded packages and laundry into the truck, another pick-up truck pulled up behind us, also now stranded. They had the back filled with wood, bolts to be split later. It was quite common for locals to find the areas that had been logged, and to glean the tops for their personal firewood. The loggers didn't mind as long as they didn't get in the way, so it was a win-win situation. Someone got free firewood, and the woods got cleaned up. This couple though, wasn't happy either about being caught with no way to cross the creek and go home. We introduced ourselves and invited them up to the house for a beer while the work on the new bridge was completed. The couple eventually became casual friends. However, years later, after Pete and I split up, the two of them became good friends of mine, and we still joke about how we met.

It was a delight having the new bridge, a good, solid way to cross the creek. It was welded steel I-beams buried into the banks, 4" × 12" × 20' treated boards, all wide enough and sturdy enough for their logging trucks. I met with the logger, the boss I had yelled at, and apologized for my outburst. Then I asked politely for one minor adjustment to that new bridge. They had placed the second layer of stabilizing boards to fit the wide axel of the trucks, and my Jeep didn't ride evenly across them. He was more than happy to add one more row of boards for me.

BITS AND PIECES

BASIC WHITE SAUCE

This was one of the first things I ever mastered in the kitchen. It has many uses and endless variety.

A roux (pronounced rue) is a mixture of butter or other fat and flour, cooked together. The roux is the thickening agent in sauces. Some recipes call for a dark roux, which is achieved by cooking the butter longer so it darkens; most of my recipes will call for a light roux. I highly recommend using a wire whip for stirring. This is supposed to be a very smooth sauce and a whip will give you the best results.

The recipe is very simple and very easy to remember.

This will give you a thin, creamy sauce.

- 1 T. butter
- 1 T. flour
- 1 cup milk

FOR A THICKER SAUCE:

- 2 T. butter
- 2 T. flour
- 1 cup milk
- *Salt and pepper to taste is always an option, depending on your dietary restrictions.

Melt the butter in a saucepan. When it begins to bubble, add the flour and stir with a wire whip over low heat. When the roux begins to bubble again, or when the flour is well incorporated, add one half cup of the milk. Again, stir constantly over low heat. As it begins to thicken, add the rest of the milk and stir until thickened.

The variations come with what is added.

Béchamel Sauce: While melting the butter, add 2 T. finely chopped onions and sauté, then proceed. For a smooth Béchamel, strain out the onions.

Alfredo Sauce: Stir in ½ cup shredded Parmesan cheese at the end. Other shredded cheeses can be used and will give a different taste.

One more option: To a basic white sauce, adding some raw, chopped shrimp, crab, or lobster will produce a delightful sauce for vegetables or pasta. Once the seafood is added and heated, allow it to sit for 30 minutes for the flavor to penetrate the sauce.

Once you have the white sauce made, experiment. A béchamel with some cheese stirred in and shrimp added served on top of pasta is a very tasty and satisfying meal.

Gravy and white sauce are very similar. With a white sauce, the liquid is added to the thickener, and with gravy the thickener is added to the liquid. White sauce uses milk, gravy uses broth. Once you have mastered one, you have mastered both. They are both smooth and delicious!

For a table presentation, garnish the bowl of white sauce with snips of parsley or chives.

VERSATILE SPICE BLENDS

PEPPER BLEND #1

This blend of herbs and spices is very versatile and can be used on almost anything from meat to fish, even vegetables. Whole spices (and pepper is a spice!) last so much longer than anything pre-ground and taste much better, too.

- 2 T. peppercorns
- 2 tsp. *each* oregano, basil, and rosemary
- 2 tsp. coarse pink salt
- 2 tsp. garlic powder
- ¼ tsp. crushed red pepper flakes

I have a coffee mill I use only for fresh grinding spices, I suggest you get one. Add the peppercorns and pulse to grind the pepper. Add the rest and pulse again to blend. This blend is easy to double or even triple, and stores very well in a dry container inside a dark cupboard.

This blend is ideal for meat, such as beef or venison. Can also be used for chicken.

PEPPER BLEND #2

- 1 T. peppercorns
- 1 tsp. coarse pink salt
- ½ tsp. celery seed
- 4 bay leaves
- ½ tsp. brown or yellow mustard seeds
- 2 whole cloves
- 2 tsp. paprika

Using the coffee mill, grind the peppercorns first. Add the rest and grind again until everything is almost a powder.

This blend is great for fish, seafood, or chicken.

PICKLING SPICES

- 2 T. mustard seed
- 1 T. whole allspice
- 2 tsp. coriander
- 1 tsp. red pepper flakes
- 1 t. ground ginger
- 1 bay leaf, crumbled
- 1 stick cinnamon, broken into pieces
- 2 whole cloves

Add the first two in a jar and shake. Add the next and shake. Continue adding one at a time and shaking, until all are in the jar.

DIJON MUSTARD

The basic recipe is very simple. Take two tablespoons of mustard seeds and crush (I prefer to use my herb/spice mill). Place the powder in a small bowl and add two tablespoons of water. Allow to chill overnight for the flavor to develop. Careful – this is not your plain yellow mustard; it will be hot, like a dijon! If it's too thick, thin with a bit of water.

The variations are simple: use whatever liquid you want. Beer is a good choice and so is wine or ACV. Try the different varieties; you may never go back to store bought mustard.

MAYONNAISE

Yes, real mayonnaise! Rich, sinful, and definitely not low-cal.

- 2 egg yolks
- Salt and white pepper to taste
- 1 tsp. dried mustard or fresh made, page 189
- 1 tsp. white vinegar or lemon juice
- 1 cup olive oil

Place eggs in a bowl, add salt, pepper, vinegar, and mustard. Beat constantly with a wire whisk while adding oil, a few drops at a time. If not to be used immediately, stir in a teaspoon of water to help stabilize the egg yolk. Keep chilled.

CATSUP

This is my sister's recipe. I don't know where she got it, but we love it.

- 14 pounds ripe tomatoes
- 2 onions
- ¼ tsp. cayenne pepper (½ tsp. if you like your catsup zippy)
- 1½ cup apple cider vinegar
- 2 sticks cinnamon, broken
- 1 T. whole cloves
- 3 cloves garlic, finely chopped or mashed
- 1 T. paprika
- 1 cup sugar
- 1 T. salt

Wash the tomatoes, cut in quarters, and place in a large pot. Peel onion, quarter, and add to tomatoes. Cook until very soft, and run through a food mill. Place the strained tomatoes in a pot. Add the cayenne pepper and cook rapidly to about one half the original volume.

Place the cinnamon, cloves, and garlic in a spice bag, or tie in a piece of cheesecloth and add to the tomatoes. Add remaining ingredients and cook with a rapid boil until it reaches the desired consistency, stirring frequently. Remove spice bag.

Pour into hot pint or half-pint jars. Attach lids and rings. Process in a boiling water bath for 15 minutes. Makes approximately three pints or six half pints.

BBQ SAUCE

- 1 pint plain tomato sauce
- ¼ cup brown sugar, honey, or maple syrup
- 1/8 cup vinegar
- 2 T. Dijon mustard
- 2 T. Worcestershire
- 1 tsp. liquid smoke
- ½ tsp. salt
- ½ tsp. black pepper
- ½ tsp. garlic powder
- 1 T. dried onion

Mix all the ingredients together and simmer on low until it reaches the consistency you prefer. This will keep a month when kept cool, but it's usually gone before then.

GARLIC OIL

I use this for so many of my recipes that I forget to even mention it. Just put all ingredients in a pint jar and keep it in the refrigerator. To use, bring it to room temperature and stir before using.

- 1 pint of olive oil
- 4 garlic cloves, cleaned and sliced in half
- Basil leaves and/or a sprig of fresh rosemary, optional

Use any time you need oil for sautéing or on salads.

JERKY MARINADE

When there is extra venison, a great way to preserve it is to make jerky. A nutritious snack that doesn't need refrigeration when you're out in the woods hunting, sitting in a boat fishing, or any time.

The meat is thinly sliced, no thicker than one half inch, and marinated, completely submerged in the liquid for 24-48 hours, then dried.

In a three quart pail mix:

- 4-5 cloves of garlic, minced or smashed
- 1-2 small onions sliced or a bunch of chives
- ½ cup brown sugar or maple syrup
- 1 cup soy sauce
- ½ cup teriyaki sauce
- ½ cup vinegar

Add the meat in small batches, mixing by hand, making sure it is all well coated. Add some water if needed to have the meat covered. If there is a lot of meat, double the ingredients.

To dry, shake the solids off the meat and lay on a dehydrator rack. Be sure the meat does not touch; you want the pieces to dry evenly. Drying time will vary depending on the thickness of the meat. Follow the directions of your dryer unit.

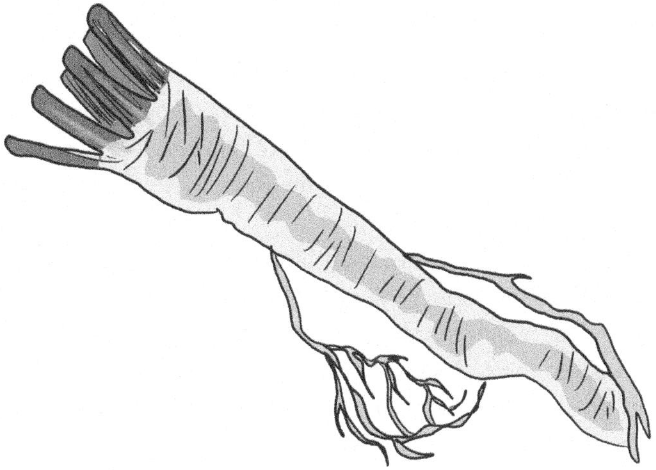

MAKING HORSERADISH

I love horseradish, in small amounts. Freshly made from the garden, this condiment is a great deal stronger than store bought. It's easy to grow, just remember to plant it where you want it to stay forever. It's very difficult to move once established, much like mint and comfrey. I have dug some up, thinking I got that entire root, only to find it growing again in that same spot. Just be warned.

At the beginning of my first novel, *Cracked Earth*, I related my first attempt at making horseradish. It was a learning experience even though it was comical. The steps are: dig, wash, peel, shred/chop, season. Simple? Yeah, right.

Dig your roots in the fall after the leaves have dried or at least wilted, depending on your seasons. Cut all remaining leaves off and soak in a pail or deep bowl of water. If you're going to go through all the steps to do this, I suggest you make a big batch, enough to last you.

After soaking the dirt off for an hour or so, scrub the root with a brush under running water, breaking the root apart if necessary to get at all the soil that has clung.

Now is the time to put on rubber gloves, a mask and goggles. (Note: the mask may or may not be necessary at this point depending on the pungency.) Using a sharp paring knife, carefully peel the outer skin off; set aside the roots in another bowl of water. Rinse well and cut into one inch pieces.

Now comes the fun part, and I highly recommend you do this outside on a nice day. Set up a table outside for your food processor. (Note: Shredding by hand can be done, but it's very time consuming and you're more exposed to the fumes.) Using the finest shredding blade you have, shred all of those pieces. When you are finished, **BE VERY CAREFUL** when you take the lid off, as the fumes are very strong. This is the part where you might want to add goggles to the mask and gloves! Dump the horseradish into a bowl and immediately cover. Replace the shredding blade with the chopping blade and return mixture to the processor. Pulse several times to get a fine consistency. Add one quarter cup of vinegar at a time (I prefer my own Apple Cider Vinegar) and pulse again to blend until you get the 'wetness' you prefer. Put it back into the bowl and cover. Leave the bowl outside and bring all else in to rinse in cold water. You can wash now or later.

Prepare your jars. I have found that half pint canning jars are the best size. Wash the jars in hot soapy water and let drain until you need them. Sterilize the lids. When you're done making the horseradish, take the jars outside and fill them, wiping the rims and securing the lids and rings. Take inside and wash the outside of the jars. This will keep a very long time since the vinegar is a preservative. The most important part is to remember **DO NOT** touch your face, eyes, nose, or any open cut at any time during this whole process!

SAUSAGE

Making your own sausage can be fun and very rewarding. Although they are nice to have, you don't need a 'stuffer'—just make patties. You can make this with all pork, all beef, half pork – half beef or half pork – half venison. Because venison is a dry meat, I discourage you from making sausage with all venison. Since this recipe is for using fresh or freezing, you can 'play' with the amounts some. Even the small amount of garlic used here will be enhanced by the curing time, so increase a little at a time. Fry a small patty after the 24 hours and taste. Increase seasonings at this time if you like. You do not have to cure a second time.

ITALIAN STYLE SAUSAGE:

- 5 lbs. pork, ground medium
- 1 large onion, finely chopped
- 1 T. crushed garlic (5 cloves)
- 2½ tsp. fennel seed
- 1 tsp. paprika (½ t. if using Hungarian hot)
- 1 tsp. cayenne pepper
- 2 T. oregano
- 1 tsp. salt
- 8 T. water

Mix meat with water. Mix spices together first and then add to the meat. Mix thoroughly. Wrap tightly or place in a large zipper-type bag. Keep well chilled for 24 hours. Make patties and freeze or cook. It's that simple.

KIELBASA STYLE SAUSAGE:

- 2 ½ lbs. *each* pork and beef or venison coarsely ground
- 3 T. mustard seed
- 1 T. crushed garlic (5 cloves)
- 1 T. salt
- 1 T. fresh coarsely ground pepper
- 8 T. water

Follow the directions for Italian sausage above.

PICKLED SAUSAGE

I once came across a sale on Polish Kielbasa, which I just love. I bought seven packages and used a standard pickling recipe for preserving them. It's easy to eat a whole jar, they are that good.

- 2 lbs. precooked kielbasa (or any type of precooked sausage, even cocktail wieners)
- 1 small onion, thinly sliced

BRINE:

- 1 cup water
- ¾ cup brown sugar
- 3 cups white vinegar
- 1 tsp. crushed red pepper flakes
- 1 T. pickling spices

Cut up the sausage into three inch pieces and put into jars with a few slices of onion. (I prefer using wide mouth jars.)

Bring the brine to a boil and simmer 5 minutes.

Pour hot brine into jars and put lid/ring on hand tight. At this point they can be put in the refrigerator to cure or they can be processed in a boiling water bath canner for 20 minutes. If in the refrigerator, allow to pickle at least two days and it will keep for several weeks.

DEVILED EGGS

My brother's wife gave me the secret to cooked eggs that shell easily: steam. I no longer boil eggs, I steam them for 10 minutes and even after chilling, the shells slide right off. Having a lot of eggs from the chickens, I'm always looking for different ways to prepare them. This method of cooking gives a clean and appealing looking egg. I have a large vegetable steamer that will hold eighteen eggs, however the small basket style will work just as well for six eggs. Remember to cool them to handling temperature.

Slice cooked eggs lengthwise and remove yolk. Set the whites on a platter or in a deviled egg tray. Mash the yolks in a bowl; add garlic salt and pepper to taste; toss. Add one green onion, finely chopped and toss again. Mix in two tablespoons of mayonnaise and one tablespoon of milk. If it isn't moist enough for your taste, add more milk, a little at a time until it is. Mix well.

If you have a pastry bag and star tip, pipe the yolk mixture into the whites. If not, then spoon the yolks in. Garnish with bits of dill.

FILLING VARIATIONS:

Up here, we have inexpensive Whitefish caviar available that is delicious. Many times I have used this instead of the yolks for a healthier dish. Or mix the caviar with sour cream, plain yogurt, or even small curd cottage cheese. Garnish this with dill also.

Another wonderful filling is hummus.

GARNISH VARIATIONS:

I've used garnish to differentiate what's in the filling. A close friend doesn't like onions, so I make a batch without and garnish those with dill and the onion ones with chives.

Sliced olives, green or black, make a good garnish, as does bits of roasted red peppers, slivers of tomato, parsley, or a dash of paprika or chili powder, anything that adds color.

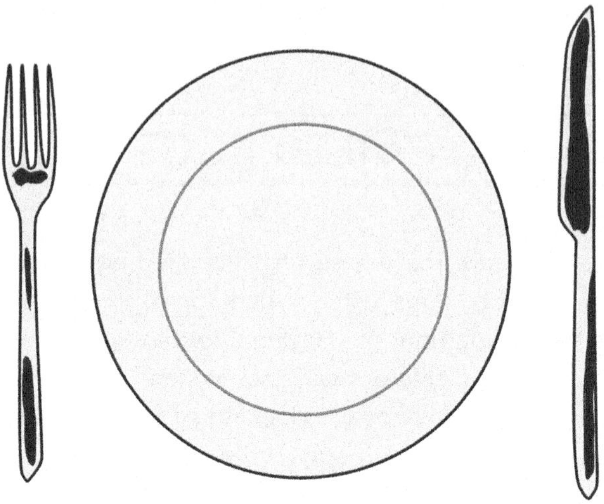

A TYPICAL TWO WEEK MENU IN THE FALL

Oct. 17	Pasta w/mustard sauce, zucchini, patty pan and wild mushrooms and a salad.
Oct. 18	Venison pasties w/brown gravy. Salad
Oct. 19	Spinach crepes and fresh carrots
Oct. 20	Lasagna and Caesar salad, garlic bread sticks
Oct. 21	Angel hair pasta w/pesto and tomatoes
Oct. 22	Turkey stroganoff, fried green tomatoes
Oct. 23	Whiskey steak w/mushrooms and egg and cheese pasta
Oct. 24	Swedish wheat balls, green beans, salad
Oct. 25	Spinach and cheese pinwheels on red pepper sauce
Oct. 26	Dijon chicken breasts on rice; spiced beets
Oct. 27	Walnut ravioli w/gorgonzola sauce; Caesar salad
Oct. 28	Cannelloni w/chicken, spinach, mozzarella cheese; salad
Oct. 29	Eggplant pasta w/tomato sauce
Oct. 30	Stuffed rolled venison roast, corn, fresh rolls
Oct. 31	Chicken paprikosh w/fresh noodles, carrots
Nov. 1	*Special Dinner* "We're ready for Winter Dinner" Shrimp cocktail, Caesar salad, grilled salmon, foil wrapped potatoes and apple pie

CARROT JELLO

For garnishing your plate, prepare orange jello according to the package. Stir in one cup finely shredded raw carrots. Pour into a long, flat container so the jello is only one half inch deep. Chill until set. Cut into three inch squares and serve on a lettuce leaf as a colorful addition to any meal. This also brings back many fond memories of my mother's cooking.

VINEGARS

APPLE CIDER VINEGAR (ACV)

Apple Cider Vinegar (ACV) is one of the best kept kitchen secrets! Not only is it great to use in cooking and on salads, but it can be used as a wash for cleaning vegetables and fruit, and it will disinfect the countertops.

All it takes to make it is pure, fresh apple cider and patience.

Whatever container you use, be sure it is full to the neck. Since cider is made only once a year, I make two one gallon containers for my yearly supply. The steps are easy. First you turn the cider into wine by allowing it to ferment. The apples have a natural yeast on the skin so you don't have to add anything except a bubble cap or a balloon. I recommend the bubble cap. Watch the cap to be sure there is always water in it as you don't want air to get in – yet. When the bubbling slows down, you are close to having wine. At this point, remove the bubble cap and attach a square of cheesecloth folded several times. You want air to get in now, but nothing else. The wine starts to ferment again, but it will sour because of the air. Keep it covered for four to six months. When it has reached the taste you like, put a regular cap on it and store it in the pantry. You're done!

RAMP VINEGAR

For this I use the bulbs only, and regular mouth pint jars. Sterilize the jars according to directions in a book on canning. Fill the jar half full of ramp bulbs, and fill the rest of the way with vinegar, either white or ACV. Attach a lid and ring. A ten minute water bath is all that is needed to seal the jar.

BLUEBERRY VINEGAR

This might sound strange, but you don't eat the blueberries! This vinegar adds a light, slightly fruity bite to salads.

Fill a pint canning jar with blueberries, pressing down to pack and to release juices. Top the jar off with vinegar. White vinegar is preferable, but any vinegar will do. Cap the jar and store in a cool dark place for one month. Strain into a second jar and discard the berries.

GARLIC-BASIL VINEGAR

Thread four whole cloves of garlic onto a wooden skewer, alternating with several whole leaves of basil. Place in a pint jar and cut the skewer off to fit. Fill with any vinegar. Cap the jar and store in a cool dark place for one month. Remove skewer and use in any salad.

TARRAGON-ROSEMARY VINEGAR

Select a branch of fresh tarragon and remove any brown or discolored leaves. Repeat with fresh rosemary. Place both herbs in a pint jar and fill with vinegar. The herbs may be left in for a stronger flavor, or refill with vinegar as you use it. Use in any recipe that calls for vinegar.

CANNING BACON

Many years ago, bacon could be purchased rolled up in a tall metal can. It was easy to store and tasted wonderful. I haven't found any in many, many years, so I set about to can my own.

To can one pound of bacon you must use a pressure canner, wide mouth quart jars, and parchment paper. I learned the hard way. With a regular mouth canning jar, the bacon is very difficult to get in and out. If waxed paper is used it will disintegrate during the processing. I also highly recommend using thick cut bacon, as regular cut tends to fall apart, although it is still quite edible.

Let the bacon come to room temperature.

Lay a large sheet of parchment paper on your work table and set the bacon in the center. Spread apart slightly with your fingers until about five inches wide.

Fold the parchment, top down, bottom up, and one side over.

Starting with the end you folded over, start to roll, not too tight, but tight enough to make the roll small enough to slide into the wide mouth jar.

Attach sterile lid and band.

Process for pork/meat, 90 minutes @10# pressure. Adjust to your altitude.

Bacon will be soft, as it is sitting in its own grease, but it will be fully cooked by the canning process.

To use, unroll, peel off however many slices you want, and crisp to taste in fry pan.

FIRST BLIZZARD

The curtain of white
Falling, drifting
Billowing in the wind
Blinding to what lies
Beneath or beyond

The forecast the night before called for 6-8 inches of snow. Not anything the four-wheel drive Jeep couldn't handle with ease. It was parked about halfway to the house instead of out by the main road. Loggers were working between us and the county road, and agreed to keep us plowed out to that prearranged point. It was a good arrangement for everyone. My car wasn't in the way of their big trucks, and it wasn't so far to snowshoe out.

A week or two earlier, the generator had failed and was now in the repair shop. The generator's primary function was to pump the deep well, and without it, there was no water for the holding tank. This was not a big issue, just an inconvenient one. We lived without running water for four months when we first moved here. But that was in the summer. There is an artesian spring about two miles up the county road that runs all year around, never freezes, never runs dry. As I did back in the beginning, I began to make regular trips to the spring to fill five gallon containers. I would snowmobile to the car, load up the containers, and drive to the spring. Since I could melt snow for washing and flushing, five gallons lasted longer.

It was Wednesday night and Pete and I agreed that 6-8 inches on top of a plowed road wasn't enough to worry about moving the car further out, even if the loggers didn't come back until Monday. So I settled into bed, with one more thing on my chore list for the next day.

By morning, though, there was already 12" of new snow and we were in a near whiteout condition. So much for accurate weather forecasts. The major thing facing me was that we needed water. If it hadn't been for that, I would have never even put my boots on. The radio was now calling for a Winter Storm Warning, with heavy accumulation and additional 'lake effect' snow possible. Seems there had been a wind shift, and it was now coming off Lake Superior. I knew the Jeep should be moved, but 12" might be pushing it. The decision was to run the snowmobile out to the county road a few times to create a path for the Jeep. This was also the year Pete's back was giving him trouble and he could not risk the jarring ride of the snowmobile. I had to go, even though I was new to handling the snowmobile I had purchased only weeks before. I was confident. I was tough. I was terrified.

As I rounded the curve in the road approaching the area where the car was parked, I knew it was going to be difficult. Even though the snowmobile was fairly new, a long track model and supposedly capable of wondrous feats of travel, Pete told me never to stop in really deep snow - I might not get going again. I passed the Jeep, buried deep in snow and drifts, and headed toward the bridge.

The logging bridge crossed the creek, a small river actually, and the road then had significant slopes on either side. With snow falling fast and more snow being blown upward in my face by the sled, I started the downward slope to the bridge. A quick glance to the other side almost took my breath away. There was no definition in the road at all. It had completely filled in from drifting, which meant there was much more snow than a mere 12". I crossed the bridge at the moderate speed I felt was safe, and with my mate's advice in my mind, began a mantra of *"Don't stop. Don't stop. Don't stop."* I aimed between the trees where I knew the road was somewhere beneath all that snow, and gave the sled as much gas as I could and still maintain control. I was enveloped in a cloud of icy white. I drove blindly for what felt like an eternity, and in reality was maybe five seconds. I was now at the top, next to Three Shoes Camp, in an area where the loggers had recently plowed, and once again had only 12" beneath me. I felt giddy with success, yet overwhelmed that I'd have to do it again going back. I continued toward the county road, slowing to my normal speed but never stopping. I would turn around and go back home. The Jeep wasn't going anywhere today... and I shouldn't have either.

At another curve in the road, there was someone plowing. Maybe I would get the Jeep out after all. After a few words with the young man at the wheel, he headed for the bridge. It was interesting to note that he was plowing as he went - without dropping the blade. Not a good sign, but then I knew the snow was deep. I turned around and waited in the plowed area, not wanting to get in his way. I waited, and waited. He should have been back by now. I slowly moved the snowmobile forward, being very conscious that he might not be able to see me through the blowing snow. A few hundred yards more and I saw him... walking. He had gotten the truck stuck next to the Jeep. His plan was to walk out and hitch a ride. Having just turned around at the main road, I knew the county plows hadn't been by and there was no traffic whatsoever. Even his recent tire tracks were no longer visible. I convinced him to come home with me and use the cellular phone to call someone. I had never driven someone before, and I had only been solo sledding for two weeks

His name was Gordy. A nice young man, fair haired, blue eyed, typical Finnish looks, mid-twenties, friendly, funny, intelligent, and turns out he was the logging company forester, which means he was the boss in the field. A good person to know when there was logging going on all around us.

Gordy warmed up by the cookstove, had something warm to drink, and called his crew to come get him. Since the Jeep wasn't going anywhere for several days, I decided to load up the five gallon containers on the detachable sled I use and go to the spring on the snowmobile. There certainly wouldn't be any vehicle traffic for me to worry about today. I took Gordy back to his truck and continued out to the road.

There may not have been any traffic to be concerned about, but it was still one of the most nerve wracking rides I've ever made. The plows still hadn't been by and the snow was getting deeper by the minute. When I approached the spring, I realized I couldn't turn around. Although the snowmobile had reverse, backing up in deep snow would only bury the treads. I had to continue almost another mile to an area where I knew there would be adequate room to make a circle. I still had some maneuvering to do, but finally got going in the right direction.

When I pulled up to the spring, I realized I hadn't seen another person the entire time, hadn't heard another sound, not even another snowmobile. I left the sled running in the middle of the road and filled four containers, strapping them down when I was finished. I prayed that extra 150 pounds being pulled wouldn't bog me down too much. I had to go even slower to keep the attached sled from fishtailing and tipping over. Halfway back to my road, I was passed by two snowmobiles. Now *that* didn't surprise me. Snowmobilers around here are fanatics, and drive way too fast for me. They left me in a spray of snow, blinded once more. I believe in wearing a helmet, but the snow was falling so fast I couldn't keep my visor cleared and had to push it out of my way. My face was quickly getting numb.

Back on my logging road I breathed a little better and felt my anxiety lessen. I was in familiar territory. Gordy was still digging around his truck, using a way too small shovel, wondering where his rescuers were. After explaining the conditions on the county road, it didn't take much convincing to have him join us again back at the house. He was cold, wet, and approaching hypothermia. With the additional weight on the seat, the traveling was actually a little smoother.

Gordy helped me unload the water, and then stood shivering by the cookstove, trying to warm up. I hung his damp jacket and gloves by the stove to dry. Another phone call revealed the crew answering his first call had been stopped by the county and sent back - to get a bigger truck. An hour or so passed, a few more calls, another cup of coffee and dry clothes, and Gordy was ready to try again. The young man was undaunted by all the snow, but then, he was born here, and this was only Pete's and my second winter. I found a thick pair of hunting socks for Gordy to use. He slid his feet back into his still wet leather work boots, boots that were fine for walking in the woods, but not meant to stay dry in deep snow. I had shown him to wrap his feet in plastic baggies to keep the wetness away from the dry socks. I did warn him that lasts for only a while, and then it seeped through. With his knit hat pulled low over his ears, insulated canvas jacket zipped high, dry gloves, and soggy shoes, he followed the snowmobile trail back out to his truck. His back disappeared from my sight within a few yards. I found out later that by the time he walked back to his half buried truck, his feet were wet again. I felt badly that I hadn't driven him out, but the two trips had exhausted me and I was now paranoid about getting stuck. I figured I had used up my good luck for the day, maybe for the week.

The snow stopped sometime on Friday. The official total was 40" in less than 36 hours. Up in the hills where we were, it was much, much deeper. The blowing and drifting made it worse. It had brought the county to a standstill. That is still the worse storm I've seen to hit here.

I saw Gordy again later that summer and he told me how long he'd had to wait for someone to get him. Hindsight told me we should have just given him a beer and dinner and had him spend the night, to worry about escape the next day.

Come to think of it, he still has my socks!

Thank you for reading my cookbook and my stories. I've lived an interesting life and I'm happy I could share some of it with you. I will leave you with one last elegant and delicious dessert:

GRILLED PEARS

I prefer red pears for this but any type will do. Slice a pear in half lengthwise and remove the core. Grill cut side down until heated through, approximately 10 minutes over medium heat. Turn cut side up and grill an additional 5 minutes.

Pour two tablespoons of thick cream on a small plate in a circle and set the pear in the center. Dust the pear with a few grindings of fresh black pepper. Yes, black pepper! Fill the bowl of the pear with more cream, and then drizzle maple syrup back and forth across the pear and the plate.

Serves 2.

Option: instead of maple syrup, drizzle melted chocolate.

Enjoy!

ABOUT THE AUTHOR

Deborah started writing short stories when she was 13 and she made her first loaf of bread at 16. In *A Prepper's Cookbook* she has combined her talents of writing, teaching, and cooking. Deborah is also the author of the survival series *The Journal*.

Deborah D. Moore resides in a quiet, cozy, forested corner of the Upper Peninsula of Michigan with her cat Tufts.

Made in United States
Orlando, FL
24 June 2022

19116172R00124